POETICA 4

Flower and Song

T0159758

By Edward Kissam

POETRY

The Sham Flyers   1969
Jerusalem and The People   1972
The Arabs   1972

By Michael Schmidt

POETRY

The Resurrection of the Body   2006
Collected Poems   2009

TRANSLATIONS

On Poets & Others, Octavio Paz   1991

LITERARY HISTORY AND CRITICISM

Lives of the Ancient Poets: The Greeks   2004
Lives of the Poets   1998

Flower and Song

Poems of the Aztec Peoples

Translated and introduced by

Edward Kissam
and
Michael Schmidt

ANVIL PRESS POETRY

Second edition published in 2009
by Anvil Press Poetry Ltd
Neptune House 70 Royal Hill London SE10 8RF
www.anvilpresspoetry.com
First edition published in 1977

ISBN 978 0 85646 423 2

This book is published
with financial assistance from
Arts Council England

A catalogue record for this book
is available from the British Library

Designed and set in Monotype Walbaum by Anvil
Printed and bound in Great Britain
by Hobbs the Printers Ltd

UNESCO COLLECTON OF REPRESENTATIVE WORKS
MEXICAN SERIES

This book has been accepted in the Literature Translation Series of
the United Nations Educational, Scientific and Cultural Organization
(UNESCO)

...and the paintings with which they kept their records are gone, because [the conquerors] ... burnt them in the royal palaces of Nezahualpitzintli, in a great apartment which was the central archive of their papers, where all their ancient heritage was painted; which today their descendants lament with great sorrow, for they remain as in darkness, without record or memory of the deeds of their ancestors.'

JUAN BAUTISTA POMAR
Relación de Tezcoco
(1582)

Acknowledgements

Versions by Michael Schmidt first appeared in *Antaeus*, *Carcanet*, *Journals of Pierre Menard*, *New Measure* and *The Island*; versions by Edward Kissam in *Alcheringa*, *Anonym*, *Antaeus*, *Bricoleur*, *A Curriculum of the Soul* (fasc. 13), *Prairie Schooner*, *Shaking the Pumpkin* (ed. Jerome Rothenberg, Doubleday, 1972) and *The Sham Flyers* by Edward Kissam (Anvil, 1969).

I should like to thank Alfred Bush who supplied me with texts that were otherwise unavailable. – E. K.

Contents

Note on Pronunciation   *page* 8

Introduction   9

1   **Songs of Life** (poems 1–46)   23

2   **Ritual Songs** (poems 47–67)   63

3   **Myths and Legends** (poems 58–62)   79

4   **Songs of War** (poems 63–83)   97

Appendix: Poems from Contemporary Oral Tradition

    Four Otomí poems   119

    Six Lacandon poems   120

    Huichol Shaman chants   124

Afterword BY EDWARD KISSAM   131

Afterword BY MICHAEL SCHMIDT   137

Glossary   143

Sources   155

References   156

Further Reading   159

Note on Pronunciation

As a rough guide, Aztec names are pronounced as though written in Spanish, with the following exceptions:

ll is a double *l* as in 'soul love'
x is pronounced much as *sh* in English
c is pronounced as English *k*
h in *hu* and *ha* is pronounced as English *w*
terminal *h* is pronounced as the *h* in English 'how'
n nasalizes the preceding vowel as in French 'on'
i is rather closer to English *ee* as in 'feet' than to *i* in Spanish

Two recurring proper names are Ipalnemoani (*I*-pal-ne-*moa*-ni) and Tamoanchan (Ta-mo-*an*-chan), where italics indicate the stressed syllables. Generally, primary stress falls on the first syllable of a word, and in compound words a secondary stress is evident in the first syllable of the second word-component, e.g. *Nez*ahual-*co*yotl.

Introduction

Smoke rises, the mist
is spreading.

Weep, my friends,
and know that by these deeds
we have forever lost our heritage.

THIS VALEDICTION concludes one of the last Aztec poems, composed when the Spaniards were beginning their wholesale suppression of native culture in Mexico in 1521. The poem laments the fall of the great island capital of the Aztecs, Tenochtitlan, the warriors' flight across the lake, and their premonition of a total loss of their heritage in the face of the brutal, mysterious conquerors. The Aztec empire, already under strain before Cortés arrived, was simply snuffed out – and worse, the palaces and temples, the schools and ceremonial centres, with all that they contained of artefacts and archives, were pillaged, burnt out, or razed systematically. The Aztecs blamed their own cowardice for their defeat – but more than cowardice was involved. The strange men with guns and horses seemed to have stepped out of vital legend: native astrologers had long predicted some such advent. The Aztec empire was in decay, and even had Spain not come, Tenochtitlan, with its warring sun-cult of Huitzilopochtli-Tonatiuh and its expansionist dreams, was vulnerable to its own flaws – its military and administrative over-extension, its unpopularity, its institutional weaknesses. Nonetheless, the traumatic sudden loss of all that they had built and made, and the consequent relentless suppression of all that they had thought and discovered, amounted to the extermination of a rich and complex culture, not merely another modification of the Aztec power structure. Previously tribe had built on tribe, culture on culture, and each

9

had learned from its predecessors the lessons of science, art and social relations. This was the end of a long evolutionary process towards a sophisticated native society with its roots in a rich tradition. One of the last poets laments:

> *In grief we beat our fists*
> *against the walls of our mud houses,*
> *a net of holes our only heritage.*

In their origins, the Aztecs were a nomad tribe from northern Mexico. Their rapid ascent to power in less than a century, and the opulence of the great capital of their empire led to a heavy investment in asserting, often via revisionist history, their cultural and spiritual superiority to their vassals. They were the chosen of the Sun. Their function was to keep the sun in circuit. Their world was the fifth creation, theirs the fifth Sun. The previous creations had each been destroyed by elemental forces. This fifth was equally vulnerable – a precarious balance, a delicate tension between the four elements and the four cardinal directions. The myth of the five creations was inherited from previous cultures. The Aztecs, however, saw themselves as actively involved in the play of elements, maintaining the fifth sun: it had to be sustained and nourished with human strength – by the 'flowered war' which led to the recruitment of sacrificial victims, whether for the gift to the sun of living hearts, or for the transmission of human energy to the Sun by flaying sacrificial victims, where the priest donned the skin of the flayed man and danced to Huitzilopochtli-Tonatiuh, the god of war, the sun. This was the ceremony of Xippe Totec.

This grotesque ceremonial, the Aztecs' addition to an inherited mythology and structure of rituals, was dictated as much by political necessity as by religious zeal. Conquest meant that thousands of prisoners were brought back from the wars to the capital. The state could ill tolerate the threat of so large a body of alien, hostile men in the heart of its capital, while its armies were off annexing more territory or pacifying tribes already annexed. Furthermore, it was an irritating expense to feed and house prisoners. Better to be rid of them – and how better to justify their disposal, and to justify the wars, than to call each action holy, to harness religion in the service of imperial ambitions? The Sun's elected tribe found it easy to accept this extension of the myth, referring all their military action to the sun cult, reducing war and sacrifice to grand and potent ritual.

A number of the poems in this anthology relate to the war cult, to the two orders of knights – 'tiger warriors' (more properly called 'ocelot warriors') and 'eagle warriors' – who are celebrated allusively. Poems with eagle and tiger imagery usually refer to the warriors in their symbolic involvement – the knights wore uniforms made of ocelot skins or of plumes, with elaborate headgear. Other military references, tribal and symbolic, are explained in the Glossary. Not all the war poems celebrate the battle or the faith – some lament the loss of kin and friend, the deceit of allies, the impersonality and apparent insignificance of the sacrifice. But the dominant strains are those of celebration and the symbolic recapitulation of specific campaigns.

Poetically, more important than the celebrations of war are the philosophical and mythological poems. These were composed by the princes and priests. The mythology of the poems derives in part from Toltec tradition – especially the references to the myth of Quetzalcoatl, the 'plumed serpent'. The Aztec authorities had done their utmost to transmute the traditions of their sophisticated ancestors – but they had not succeeded. The Toltec culture was civilized and relatively humane. Its rise had been almost as spectacularly sudden as that of the Aztecs. Its decline is cloaked in mystery. It left a tradition of crafts, of architecture and astronomy, legend and myth, to the many tribes with which it had come in contact in central and southern Mexico. The Toltec lesson was not easily forgotten – the tribe itself became a haunting legend. To the mind of Aztec and vassal princes who felt dissatisfied or disgusted with the war cult, Toltec tradition represented an alternative, a consolatory vision.

Quetzalcoatl, the 'plumed serpent' or the 'plumed twin', had been identified with one of the kings of the Toltecs – the blond god, the pale king who had taught them all they knew of heaven and earth, who as a god had, with considerable self-sacrifice, redeemed the bones of man from the underworld and remade him under the fifth Sun (poem 68). The poetry abounds with explicit and implicit allusions to him. Through him, the Toltec contribution to the Aztec poetry of 'dissent' was immeasurable. The consuming sense of the ephemerality of earthly life and pleasure, the increasing tendency to monotheism with stress on Ometeotl-Omecihuatl, the gods of duality, and Ipalnemoani, 'the one for whom all things live', in the late poems, as well as the basic humanity and the almost decadent melancholy of this alternative tradition, can be traced back in origin largely to Toltec and related legend, though what was made of the legend was highly original. And other tribal legends and cults – for instance, the fertility cults – contributed to the rich culture which subverted, in conscience at least, the war cult.

PHILOSOPHICALLY obsessed with ephemerality, depressed by the growing responsibilities of a faltering empire, and astrologically forewarned of the advent of strange visitors from another world – creatures that would emerge from legend and bring unknown visitations on the Aztec people – it can well be imagined that the Aztecs were almost anticipating the Spaniards, that they were prepared for submission. Of course, they fought. But their vassals turned on them, their king Moctezuma proved cowardly, his successor died of smallpox, their last king was tortured and executed. Then began the suppression of their culture, a suppression on the surface remarkably successful, though pockets of the old ideologies survived long after the Conquest, and vestiges of them still remain, especially in the southern and western regions of Mexico.

Fortunately, a number of the early Franciscans – first Pedro de Gante, then Andrés de Olmos, Toribío de Motolinía, and

Bernardino de Sahagún — took a systematic and remarkably modern approach to salvaging the Nahuatl language and cultural artefacts of the Valley of Mexico, developing a set of conventions for written Nahuatl and systematically bringing together fragments of the culture which was simultaneously being eradicated by others. Fray Bernardino de Sahagún must rate as the finest of the chroniclers, working with his informants to bring together volume after volume of poems, songs, and chants from the oral tradition, historical testimony, catalogues of customs and rituals, many of them preserved in sixteenth-century Nahuatl. This is how the poems in this anthology survived — in the original (albeit nuanced at least and probably distorted to some extent by the bilingual native chroniclers trained by and working in collaboration with Sahagún and other Franciscans). The large manuscript volumes were transcribed and are now published, with translations into Spanish and extensive annotations, by Angel María Garibay especially, and Miguel León-Portilla, among others. Partially, the chronicling seems to have been prompted almost by a sense of charity. Juan Bautista Pomar, one of the chroniclers, recalled the effect which the cultural extermination had on the native people in the lines from his *Relación de Tezcoco* which form the epigraph to this book.

The primary motive behind the chroniclers, however, was curiosity, and perhaps a sense that, with a clearer understanding of the minds of the people to whom they were preaching, they might better serve the purposes of conversion and education in the Roman Catholic tradition. Sahagún records that:

> *It is well known that in the caves, forests and thickets where today the damned adversary [the Devil] hides are the chants and psalms they have composed and sing to him, without understanding what is in them.*

But Sahagún was himself so in sympathy with his native informants that on two occasions his papers were confiscated.

The Spanish authorities feared his work might prove subversive back in Spain, where it was popularly believed that the Conquest had brought peace, culture and religion to a totally barbarous land.

Yet even Sahagún found his material at times obscure and unintelligible and, probably, evil in its obscurity. Only recently have we come to recognize the barriers to our understanding of non-European or 'primitive' cultures. As Claude Lévi-Strauss points out in *The Savage Mind*, 'primitive' cultures are not incapable of logical thought – they don't need it. Their world vision is not confused but fused: its habit is to see things whole, to observe the universal in the particular. This vision is different from ours, not inferior to it. But this is the main barrier which divides us from a culture not only unfamiliar but alien – a mode of thought which does not analyse and particularize but synthesizes areas and levels of experience which we would not naturally relate – except in poetry. For this reason, perhaps, our most fruitful access to Aztec thought and culture is through the poetry.

The poems we have translated are from a number of sources. *Cantares Mexicanos*, which is the source of much of the remaining poetry, includes poems from Tenochtitlan, as well as poems from Chalco, Huexotzinco, and Texcoco, city states with subtly different cultures and dialects from the Aztec. It would be more correct for us to speak of Nahuatl rather than Aztec poetry, since many of the finest poems come from cultures related to the Aztecs linguistically, but peripheral to the Tenochtitlan tradition, part of it only as tributary states are a part, culturally, of the chief state in an empire. Besides the Tenochtitlan tradition, there are two other major traditions: that of Tlaxcala and that of the Otomí nation. Even the Aztec scribe working with Olmos and Sahagún in compiling the *Cantares Mexicanos* records that the Otomí poems were unintelligible and alien to him.

The problem of obscurity in the poems is not entirely a matter of ignorance on our part. We would be grateful for more information, but obscurity is often more a matter of the Nahua poet's stylistic orientation than of our scanty information. The pervasive attitude of any nation which has made major advances of its own is one of pride: the poets of that nation take for granted certain beliefs and prejudices to which we have no access. This attitude raises other barriers between the poems and our understanding of them, if we feel that understanding includes finding them interesting as something more than mere antiquities.

In reading the poems we do not need to know the cultural tensions that gave rise to them, the rivalries of the fertility, war, and Toltec mythologies. More important to bear in mind is the fact that the poems were aristocratic. We know of no poet who was not a noble. The Aztec princes and their vassal princes were poets as a matter of course. In an oral tradition, this helps to account for the similarity of styles and the lack of personal idio-syncrasies. It also accounts – oral poetry by definition conserves traditional elements – for the subversive 'Toltec' content of some of the princes' greatest poems – justifiable enough in the case of the puppet kings, who might well feel dissatisfaction with the war cult. We can't but wonder, however, if the great war-lords, the wielders of empire, realized what they were at times saying about the fruitlessness of their activity. Perhaps, within the limits of convention, they did, and considered their utterances a ceremonial duty rather than a vital mode of expression. Or perhaps what they believed as princes and gener-als involved in 'flowered war' for the Sun did not fully satisfy them as individual men in specific human situations.

THE SPANISH CONQUEST introduced into Mexico an advanced technology, and by removing most of the motives for native initiative, ironically reinforced – especially in the southern parts of Mexico – the old 'pagan' system of thought which hundreds of missionaries had come to New Spain to stamp out. In the outlying regions, attempts to teach the natives Spanish were sporadic and inconsistent – in part because few in the populace had access to any education. Nahuatl continued to be spoken extensively and even in the first decade of the 21st century, almost 1.5 million Mexicans still speak the language and a similar number speak one of the Mayan languages. Hundreds of thousands speak one of the Mixtec languages, or Zapotec, Totonac, and another 30–40 smaller languages live on. This wavering ecclesiastical commitment to cultural assimilation allowed indigenous cultures to exist and, in some cases, retain a critical mass to thrive and evolve. Modern anthropologists have unearthed this archaic tradition among the more accessible tribes in Mexico and Central America, and some of this material is translated in the Appendix.

It is interesting in the contemporary indigenous poems to note that, when the Conquest destroyed a native system of thought which had managed to relate religion and ritual to every aspect of social life, the Amerindian societies returned to the oldest form of religious experience and expression known: individual revelation through ecstasy. This is manifested in the practice of shamanism and magic, closely associated with the religious use of psychedelic substances. Before the Conquest the idea of individual revelation had been lost, as well as the practice of medicine by a shaman to combat soul-loss or to remove magical objects from the body. But the later cultures, in their relative isolation, have evolved a religion and an oral tradition deriving much from the individual revelation of the shaman in his ecstatic state, ceremonially induced by the eating of psychedelic substances.

IN AN ORAL poetic tradition like the Aztec, technique and form are especially complex and exacting – strong rhythm, alliteration, epithets, repetition of syntactical structures and refrains being essential mnemonic devices. Aztec poetry is as complex as Celtic or Vedic oral poetry, and shares many of the devices of those traditions.

Nahuatl is a synthetic rather than an analytic language: it builds up phrases conjugated from word units and particles. Each phrase is composed of several fused elements. In a real sense, it is misleading to speak of 'words' in an oral poetic tradition. The poets spoke or sang units of meaning – bundles of sound assembled into one long phrase in which the word units were so fused as to be merely tributary elements to a single, precise symbol or meaning. Each of these complex phrases was rhythmically constructed and related to other phrases in its context alliteratively, assonantally and semantically. This quality is, of course, impossible to bring out in translation. We have tried in our lineation to reflect to some degree the phrasing effect of individual lines.

Not only is the language synthetic. So, as we mentioned above, is the vision and the process of thought – or, more precisely, inference – behind the poems. The poems have a severely restricted vocabulary, consisting mainly of flower, stone, bird, animal, war and scent imagery. Not only mnemonics prompt this limitation. Each poem relates to various levels of thought: literal, philosophical, mythical, and religious. The poetry tries to integrate these levels in a single statement, and only a small number of symbolic terms is common to all levels. The process resembles that of consistent medieval allegory, though allegory is a conscious attempt at integration, while the Aztec poems come from a tradition of fused vision and are not didactic but almost magical or visionary in the complex transcendence of their thought.

Take the word unit *xóchitl*, for example. Literally this means 'flower'. In a special Aztec construction, where two images release an abstract meaning, *in xóchitl in cuícatl* ('flower and song') means 'poetry', just as 'beauty' is sometimes rendered 'jade and lush feathers', and 'divine transcendency' becomes 'night and tempest'. *Xóchitl*, on its first symbolic level, means 'word' – the word spoken by the wise man or the singer, who is often shown in the murals and codices as emitting flowers from his mouth in complicated ascending scrolls. With reference to the solar cult, *xóchitl* comes to symbolize the heart given in sacrifice, or the warrior's heart or body given in battle, or simply blood, the body's flower. With regard to myth, it symbolizes the gift of life, the flower from the Tree of Life, and perhaps the individual *nahual* or spirit-soul. Finally, in its philosophical sense, it is the prime symbol for ephemerality. Most of the words used in the poetry have a similar transcendence of meaning — we mentioned above, for example, the images of 'eagle' and 'tiger'. In the phrases that make up the poem, each element is charged with an almost ideogrammatic complexity of meaning and must always be seen as intersecting various planes of thought. 'The body makes a few flowers / then falls away withered somewhere', one of the poems says. This can be seen as referring to the ephemerality of life, to self-sacrifice, to the creation of poems, to the generation of children.

Originality in Aztec poetry was a matter of variation on strict traditional themes, not innovation. Generally the poems are structured in stanzas, either contrasting or dialectically contradicting one another, giving the effect of internal dialogue. Or they assemble a complex of images to embody a matrix of ideas. Sahagún typified the native artists as men who 'communicate with their own hearts'.

The native metres have not been adequately explored. In translation, we have not tried to reproduce them, as they seem essentially alien to English stress patterns. The simplest metres are four-stress, usually with eight or ten syllables and generally consistent. The more meditative poems are composed in longer rhythmical runs, of twelve to fourteen syllables, with four or six stresses. Usually the line ends with a rhythmic phrase which does not contribute to the meaning (*Ohuaya, Yeehuaya, Aya*) but was probably chanted by a chorus as a refrain. Refrains are often more subtle, a phrase repeated in slightly divergent forms to give the effect of phrasal punning and to produce rhythmic unity, assonance, and rhyme. Music and dance played a large part in recitation, and we should bear this in mind while reading what are, in a sense, scores for a far more elaborate art form than simply a verbal one. We have inherited only one part of the complex ritual.

AS TRANSLATORS, we are not linguists. We have only a limited knowledge of Nahuatl, and our translations depend largely on Garibay's and León-Portilla's Spanish versions and excellent annotations of the poems. We have selected the more translatable poems and fragments, and excluded those whose obscurity makes them reluctant to cross over into English. We have provided in the Glossary explanations of the more difficult allusions.

We have tried to be true to the text and to the reader, resolving some complexities without, we hope, falsifying the tone of the poems. Undoubtedly many of the elements central to the Aztec poems have evaded our translation – but our technique in translating does, we hope, carry some of the lucidity and vitality of the originals. We have tried where possible to return to the source in human experience of the poetry. If we have been able to recreate the stance, the movement of the poems, something of them may still endure, relevant to the modern reader as once to a sophisticated audience more fully involved in the ceremony of song than most audiences before or since.

EDWARD KISSAM *and* MICHAEL SCHMIDT

1
Songs of Life

1

Shake the flower,
root out song
in your house, Ipalnemoani,
Master of Herons.
     − Rejoice!

Perhaps with words
you will be pierced, broken
to understand,
Prince Warriors:
earth is all over with.
     − Rejoice!

2

Only he, Ipalnemoani . . .
I did not know . . .
Never know him? Never know?
I was joyless among men.

You rained down joy,
your wealth and wisdom,
mercifully, Ipalnemoani,
fragrant priceless flowers.

I longed for them.
I did not know.

3

Blue birds, black birds, come
where the tree of blossoms grows —
its precious clustered leaves!
Come dark birds, blue birds,
and you, green quetzal!
 You come from Nonohualco,
the land by the water,
precious birds of Ipalnemoani.
You are his creatures. Come!

Here, in the house of moss,
spread like a flower
is the head-dress of the blue bird.
He came to contemplate the dawn.
 All your birds are waking.
The gold tzinitzcan preens,
the red quechol, the blue bird
who screams the dawn.
 Their morning
wakens you.

4

Ipalnemoani,
do you live
inside the sky?
For you hold this city
in your arms,

the land between the waters
rests on your palm.

Everywhere men pray
for you to be strong.
But you live
inside the sky
and hold this city
in your arms,
the land between the waters
rests on your palm.

5   *Place of Making*

The flower of Tamoanchan is sweet.
I offer the red flower in Tamoanchan.
        It is your heart's book,
            your song, Ipalnemoani.
You know its meaning
and its offering.
Each man finds in it his colour
and rejoices.

Your heart: your song.

Our despair is woven to a precious thing:
your song, Ipalnemoani.

6   *The Tree of Life*

Blossomed tree stands up in Tamoanchan
we were created there, we came to be there
there, the thread of our lives was strung
by the force which all things live for.

That is how I work gold,
how I polish jade,

it is the grace of my song.

It is as though it were turquoise.

It spun us around
four times
there in Tamoanchan
for which all things live.

7   *Dialogue*

i   I am come
     from the ocean
     waves
     where water is dyed
     with the morning.

ii   (I am just
     a singer.
     My heart

is a flower!
I offer – my song.)

i   I am from the rainland,
          come to please the deity!

ii   (I am just
          a singer.
          My heart
          is a flower!
          I offer – my song.)

8

Ipalnemoani,
you tint all things
with flowers,
sing them full
of colour,
whatever lives on earth.
The ties of war are broken:
only as you paint us
do we live on earth.

. . .

in the palace
still
in a jade chest
concealed
the princes can be found:
like them
we too are mortal . . .

9   *Love Song of Warriors*

They say
I am come to guard the mountain.
Ipalnemoani
paints the poet's heart
with flowers. In your palace,
Prince Tlaltecatzin,
you are alone, you sigh, lament,
you are fused with my god,
Ipalnemoani.

He is proud, your garland
draws his passion, you, the red macaw,
lovely woman, sweet mother, flower.
You lend yourself to others.
    But you will be abandoned.
    All of us
    will wither from our bodies.

Beauty!
You have come before lords,
open to love on my mat of feathers —
blue-jay, yellow parrot, quetzal feathers.
You stand there
precious, scented blossom.
You lend yourself to others.
    But you will be abandoned.
    All of us
    will wither from our bodies.

The flowering chocolate
catches fire.

We share out
the tobacco flower.
If I do not taste with my heart
I will grow drunk.

. . .

I alone am sad,
   'Why must I leave
   for the place where the bodiless dwell?
   I am a poet!
   My flowers are gold.'

I leave
and look back towards my house:
the rows of flowers . . .

. . .

Huge emeralds,
the broad fan
of quetzal plumes –
will these buy off death?

One day I leave,
go losing
myself.

Lord, I surrender!
I cry,
'Let me, the poet,
be shrouded, be gone!
Who can overcome
that destiny?'

Alone,
my heart under flowers,
I shall go.
Fine plumes are torn,
the emeralds, all precious,
will be splinters.

Let it be
to peace.

10

Here
        let our songs, our flowers
        be three
to lull our hatred,
to lull our sadness.

Friends
        rejoice: we live
        on earth briefly.
Only friendship
should fill us!

11

emeralds and
flowers fall
    like rain —

your song!
as you are
singing

in Mexico

the sun is shining!

(*Moctezuma*)

12

The butterfly
sipping:
the flower
my open heart,
friends,
a fragrant flower.

Now I scatter it
as rain.

13 *Butterfly*

What
are you thinking,
thinking,
friend?
Do you like songs?
Are you after
the flowers of God?
Rejoice among the drums!
. . . or go away, as you please.

The petal butterfly
flutters, flutters
            and tastes
the honey of our flowers.
He weaves among our sprays,
our fans and flutes, rejoicing
in our drums.
   Rejoice!

14

And what
does that sacred bird sing
where the ililin grows?

. . .

open-winged
the butterfly
wanders the flowers

to drink,
rejoice,

its open heart!
its heart a flower!

15

Flowers have come!
    to refresh
    and delight you, princes.
You see them briefly
as they dress themselves,
spread their petals,
perfect only in spring –
countless golden flowers!

The flowers have come
to the skirt of the mountain!

16

Yellow flowers,
sweet flowers,

precious vanilla flowers
the crow's dark magic flowers

weave themselves together.

They are your
flowers, god.

We only borrow them:
your flowered drum,
your bells,
your song:

they are your flowers,
god.

17

The flowers are budding,
are now beautiful
inside, in the golden hut
of the white Otomí.

You were proud of your ear-rings
of red obsidian,

you Mexicans,
there in the golden hut
of the white Otomí.

18

A beautiful pheasant sings
over the flowers
and his songs unleash
the lord of the world.

Only his own kind answer him.

Your heart is a book of paintings, singer,
you came to sing and sound your drum.

It's simply that in spring
you make men happy.

(*Nezahualcoyotl*)

19   *Song to the God of Nets and Oars*

You live by the lake, you
who nourish.

It is difficult
to feed the god.

Opochtli is my god
I must
feed him carefully
like a precious bird,

who rules
the water
it is difficult

I feed him
like a precious bird.

20

I've come this far,
to the boughs of the flowering tree.
I'm the flowered hummingbird:
I nourish myself and feel happy.
My lips taste sweet and good.

21   *Bird and Drum Song*

Rejoice, my friends: I thump the drum
and sing *totototo*
         tiquiti
         tiquiti!

Let the graceful flowers sing
in Totoquihuatzin's house
totiquiti

toti

tototoro

tiquiti

tiquiti!

My heart is jewels
tototoro
my robe of flowers is gold,
the flowers that I'll give one day
in praise!
totiquiti

toti

tototoro

tiquiti

tiquiti!

Ho! Sing the song in your heart!
tototoro
take these wreaths of roses, painted books
totiquiti

toti
which I will give one day
in homage!
totiquiti

totiquiti

tiquiti

tiquiti!

22

I come
to the patio of flowers:
my word a song
my thought a flower.
    My drumbeat
    is an open book.

I praise
        the one
        who is adored
        in every place,
        I beg his pity.
War lords, am I right
to seek him?
I, Moctezuma, am uncertain.

            Moctezuma, painter of books,
            you come
            to the patio of flowers
            to sing.
            Blue-green bird,
            you sway on your perch
            before god.
                Yellow butterfly,
                you alight!

            Moctezuma cools us
            with fans of flowers
            where we lie
            on these carpets
            woven out of leaves.

23

I come
to weave you in my chains of feathers.
I spread divans of tzinitzcan feathers,
crown you with the feathers of the bright macaw.
Brightness robes you.
In trembling green quetzal feathers
I bind you to each other,
my gathered friends!

Our love grows stronger, singing.
I carry friendship to the palaces
where we can lie content until
we journey to the dead.
Then we will have loaned
love to one another.

I come
to plant my songs,
make them grow for you.
God sent me, I possess his flowers:
my duty to weave love-chains on the earth.

(*Temilotzin*)

What were you thinking?
    Where was your heart wandering?

as you pour out your heart
as you do not hold it to a fixed direction,
you will destroy your heart,
yourself.

Are you going to extinguish yourself on earth?

Come back,
    hear the lovely song:
refresh your heart with the nectar of flowers.
They are fragrant
where my song lifts up,

I who sing to delight Ipalnemoani,
Lord of what is near and with you.

. . .

Leave the cloudy shadow,
come back with us:
raise a new song,
    as I who sing

raise up my song
to please the Lord of All Things,

if someone appears in the dwelling of your heart.

The city is spread out.
It spirals in circles of green jade,
radiating splendid light,
such plumes of paradise quetzal
are Mexico.

At the edge of the city
the boats leave and return:
the warriors.

A flowered cloud covers the people.
It is your house here,
Ipalnemoani, you rule here
and care for us.

Your song is heard in Anahuac.
It spreads over the people.
Palace of white willows,
palace of white reeds
is Mexico.

And you, as a blue heron,
spread your wings over the city,
you fly to the city. You spread
your tail and wings.
Your servants rule it all.

.   .   .

Let there be no pleasure
in wandering
lost in sadness.

Who will go to Ipalnemoani and serve him,
help him sustain heaven and earth?
His command blazes
like a bonfire.
In all four corners
dawn fires the warrior's voice.

This is the city of Moctezoma
and of Acolhuacan, of Nezahualpilli.
The throng leaves with fans of quetzal plumes,
they leave in boats, full of sighs,
full of sadness:

What will become of the city of Tenochtitlan?
What will the god decide?

26

In spring, the flowers spring up,
spread their petals
in the face of life given out.
You have an answer —
the precious spirit hummingbird
you searched for.
How many have gained
from your songs! You gave them heart.
The flowers
are moving in the wind.

(*Monencuauhtzin*)

27

Where will I go, where will I go?
Two things spring up hard, hard:
    There to your dwelling
        down
    or to the inside sky
        or here
        down
    upon the earth?

28

Your lovely song
soars easy as a hawk.
You raise it beautifully.
You are surrounded by flowers.
You sing in the flowered branches.

Are you from Ipalnemoani?
Has your god spoken to you?

You saw the dawn
and set yourself to song.

(*Ayocuan*)

29

In spring the golden corn in bloom
sets us in motion,
the cream-coloured tender ear
becomes our light;
and to know our friends' hearts
are faithful
leaves a jewel necklace
hung around our necks.

(*Ayocuan*)

30

Suffering roots in me, my song is nothing.
I'm only a squirrel skittering through the hills.
My friends are happy: maybe they're precious jade
maybe their hearts are like books, painted
with careful wisdom.
                I want them . . .

oh their song has stopped,
those who are coming from where the yucca blooms,

perhaps they are jade
perhaps their hearts are a painting.

31

I have only come to sing.
What do you say, friends?
What are you talking about here?
Here there are flowers.
The dancers, princes
come here crying out
in the middle of spring.
Unequal flowers,
slave and master's song.
In my house, all is suffering.

(*Motenehuatzin*)

White dawn, Ipalnemoani,
are we really here, talking . . .
If I were to offer you
jade green as leaves,
give you rich salves,

                 perhaps
if we invoked you
with fineries, ornaments,
the strength of fierce eagles
and fiery tigers . . .

what if no one on earth
is upright
in truth . . .

33 *Love Songs*

I am scattering
different kinds of flowers.

Here I come to give you songs
to make your head spin, flowers,
as I smile at you.

I come from where water
gushes out of the earth.
I've come to offer you songs,

flowers to make your head spin.
Oh, another kind of flower
and you know it in your heart.

I came to bring them to you,
I carry them to your house
on my back,

uprooted flowers,
I'm bent double with the weight of them
for you.

Let's go to your house, let's.

Fragrant flowers,
I bring them where you live
where the flowers open.

I offer you pleasure,
flowers I tended, flowers
carefully planted.

The fields flower for our mother.
She bathes in the sun, her feathers
open and spread.

In the house of shining books
the fields are flowering.

34

I come,
I come once more
and sing —

Listen to the song
I scatter.

My songs are known,
their fame grows
and grows,

I am flying, I'll fly
as far as Panotla.

I'm beginning,
now I can sing,
I'm from the heart of Tula,

my voice
breaks over you,
flowers open.

Listen,
listen carefully to my song.

I'm a thief of songs.

How can you
make them yours,

heart?

if you suffer,

treat it as a picture,
trace the lines,
the red and the black,

do it carefully,
draw it well

and perhaps
when they are yours

you will no longer suffer.

35

Only
for sleep we come,
for dreams.

Lie! It is a lie
we come to live on earth.

We grow like weeds
each spring,

swell green, our hearts
open,

the body makes a few flowers
and drops away withered somewhere.

36

I remember —
I came to earth
to perish from the earth.
I am Moquihuix.
Will we live
to see joy perishing?
    I wander,
everywhere I call.
    My heart lives
where the flowers,

where the songs
are spiralling.
Will we see them
perishing?

(*Moquihuix*)

37

I, who cry and suffer,
am out of my head.
Yes, I have this time, the present,
but I remember, and say

If I never died, if I were never to vanish . . .

I should go where there is no death,
where we could win some victory.

If I never died, if I never were to vanish . . .

(probably *Nezahualcoyotl*)

38

Rejoice, rejoice
my flower king:
you own many jewels —

we do not come
again:
only once
your heart knows the earth.

39

Our house on earth
we do not inhabit

only borrow it
briefly
            (be splendid, princes!)

here only
our heart sings
briefly, briefly
lent to one another

earth is not our last home:
take these flowers
            (be splendid, princes!)

40

Interwoven,
     blue and fiery flowers
your heart and word,
     prince Ayocuan.
For one instant
     make them yours
here on earth.

I cry
     because death destroys them
yes,
     destroys what we have done,
those fragile songs.

For an instant
     with the earth
make them yours.

(*Tecayehuatzin*)

I, Cacamatzin, speak
only to remember our king,
Nezahualpilli.
Does he converse
with his father king
somewhere among drums?
I remember him.

Who will not go there?
Will the man treasured as gold,
as jewels are treasured,
not go there?
Am I a shield of turquoise tiles,
will they replace the tiles that fall?
Will I become again?
be wound in fine cloth?
On earth, beside these drums,
I commemorate the kings!

(*Cacamatzin*)

42

Will Cacamatl
the eagle prince
return
or Ayocuan
whose arrow pierced the sky?
    Will he delight us again?
Not again — forever gone.

I weep for king Ayocuan,
our strongest lord.
But he has been exalted,
gone among his comrades.

    My father, my mother,
    did they know him
    on earth?

    I weep:
all are in the land
where bodies do not dwell.

43

Could it be true we live on earth?
On earth forever?

Just one brief instant here.

Even the finest stones begin to split,
even gold is tarnished,
even precious bird-plumes
shrivel like a cough.

Just one brief instant here.

(*Nezahualcoyotl*)

44

What am I to go with?
those flowers
which have closed?

Will my name be nothing some time?
Will I leave no thing behind me in the world?

At least flowers, at least songs!
How is my heart to work?

Perhaps we come, in vain, to live,
to come like springs upon dry earth.

(*Ayocuan*)

45

Don't our friends know it?
Heart hurts, is indignant
no second birth
no second time to be a son,
only once do I live in this world.

(*Tlapaltecuauhtzin*)

[Nezahualpilli, the poet-king, was Prince Cuaucuauhtzin's over-
lord. One day he fell in love with a girl Cuaucuauhtzin was raising
to be his wife. Nezahualpilli sent his vassal to war to dispose of
him and possess the girl. Before he departed, Cuaucuauhtzin
recited this poem at his farewell feast, lamenting the painful
ephemerality of friendship.]

My heart
longs for flowers.
To hold them!
My song
hurts me.
I, Cuaucuauhtzin,
long for flowers.
But I am forsaken.

Where can we flee
and not be forced to die?
If I were precious stone,
or gold, even gold,
I would be forged,
flattened on the anvil.
Only my life is my own,
forsaken.

Yoyontzin, prince,
you sound your jade drum,
your red and blue conch.
The singer stands to recite to you.
Bring sad hearts for him to relieve,
show him your sad faces here.

Let your heart spread its blossom,
let it wander the sky.
But you hate me,
forsake me to death.
I am bound to Ipalnemoani's palace,
to perish.
Perhaps you will weep for me?

You will wound your heart,
my friend. I leave
for Ipalnemoani's palace.
My heart speaks this farewell,
    'I shall not return,
      nor sprout again on earth.'
I leave you.

My labour — vain.
Friends, rejoice a while.
Will you take no pleasure
from life, my friends?

I shall carry
your beautiful flowers, your songs
with me. I never sang in spring,
but only now as I am sad,
forsaken, I, Cuaucuauhtzin.
I shall take
your beautiful flowers, your songs
with me.

(*Cuaucuauhtzin*)

2

Ritual Songs

Oh! Golden flower opens
spreads its petals, holy thighs,
her face the dark place
we were born from.
She is our mother, she's back
from where all things were born.

Oh your golden flowers!

Oh! Moist white flower opens
spreads its petals, holy thighs,
her face the dark place
we were born from.
She is our mother, she's back
from where all things were born.

She is
there on the cactus, our mother,
the dark obsidian
butterfly that gave us birth.

We saw her there
as we wandered across the endless plains,
there where she fed herself
with the hearts of deer.

She is
our mother whose body is the earth.

She is our mother,
dressed in plumes, painted white

for the sacrifice whose body will be
the earth.

Oh! In all four directions
wherever the winds blow,
the people shoot arrows in search of the gods.

Oh you became a deer in that barren land!
where those two men, Xiuhnel and Mimich,
first saw you.

48 *Song of Huitzilopochtli*

He was born on a smoking shield,
he is war,
the sun has become a warrior,
he was born
out of the belly of earth.

He was born on a smoking shield,
he is war,
the sun has become a warrior,
he was born
out of the belly of earth.

He is the first, he leads the way,
on Snake Mountain, his mask is a shield.
The sun rays splay out from it
in all four directions,
all over the world!

As he crests the ridge,
he puts on his mask, he is
the most manly of them all, the most potent.

As he shows himself,
the earth shakes and trembles,
letting loose war.
They cower before him.

Who will wear the shield of the sun's rays?
(The world the mask to cover his face.)

I came from the Seven Caves,
the first place, where magic ruled.
My footprints lead from there,
where the tribes began.

I am born. I am already born.
I was born with my cactus arrows
from the cactus which makes you drunk.

I am born. I came down as song
with my net snare ready.
I was born with my snare.
I was born with my net.

I hold it in one hand, in one
hand I hold it, with my hand.
Oh, with its hand
it will snare.

'Have I, Xochiquetzal, plumed lady of flowers,
yet left that greatest place
ruled by mist and rain?'

'Not yet.
I find myself still where I live by the river
in Tamoanchan, in the realm of spirits.'

Lord of the wind,
you have been crying,
young sun,
you search for her,
in the realm of clouds,
of turquoise, blue-green mist —

on our behalf.

In her house of clouds
in cloud banners, liquid necklaces
in water, mist, somewhere

somewhere life
in ripe wombs

Up! Come up!
Let yourself
be sent,
come out,
come,

child, feather
sub-
feathery marine
being.

Come up, come

up, come,
be born, jewel child
come up
come

Here!

Eagle, feathered mother,
circlets of blood
like jewels on her face,

feathered wounded earth
is dressed in green

spring sweeps the earth,
she rules those who sow

she is the cypress, spreading
over them, feathered wings

in our land, ears of corn
rustle, hanging on poles of bells.

Fire-hardened stick in my hand
I pierce the earth. Fire-hardened
stick in my hand

ear of corn planted in holy earth
rustles on a pole of bells.

Feathers, feathers fill my hand
ear of corn floats among bells
rustling, feathered wings.

Eagle, feathered mother
rules us, rules the roots

in earth
sprouting into leaves.

The blossom, agave, the phallic
blossom is *his* glory.

'My prince, snake, sun
fills me.'

Our mother is fierce, our mother
who fights at her lover's side.

She is the doe of Colhuacan
dressed in gentle plumage.

The sun goes to war
now the sun is going to war

men will be born and die
forever.

The doe of Colhuacan
dressed in gentle plumage.

Eagle, feathers, naked
unmasked, sun rises up
shines on her, naked
unmasked

the doe of Colhuacan
dressed in gentle plumage.

53 *Song on the Feast of Atamalcualoyan*

My heart sprouts flowers in the middle of the night.
Our mother is here, the goddess Tlazolteotl has come.

The spirit of corn was born in Tamoachan, the first place
on earth, in the realm of flowers, the first flower.

The spirit of corn was born where rain and mist rule,
where the children of man are made.

Day is going to shine, dawn will raise itself.
All the jewelled birds are sipping dew
in the realm of flowers.

On earth you stood up
in the middle of the square,
oh, Quetzalcoatl, prince.
There is happiness
beside the tree which blooms
different jewelled birds:
they become joyful.
Listen to our god speak,
listen to the jewelled birds speak!

There is no need to arm against our death.
There is no need to shoot arrows.
I must bring my flowers: the flower red as our flesh,
the white flower full of scent, from that place
where every flower blooms.

54 *Song to Xippe Totec*

You drunken cock, god, you drink the still night.
It's the blood you need to live.

Why do you deny it?

Let yourself burn,
put on your shining clothes!

Rise, shine,
god, you're sun streaming through mist
a rainbow, jade rain glistening on your back,
you're water coursing down the aqueduct, filling

you're the cypress shimmering like feathers
you're light green snaking shoots of plants

as it rains.

> 'You have done what I asked,
> the hunger is gone,
> so as to please me, so I can live.
>
> I am the shoot of corn.
> My heart is as fragile and precious as jewels
> but it waits for the rainburst,
> the gold shining through the rain.
>
> My life dawns
> on the horizon, once more
> the man who is first in war
> who comes out first to do battle

is born.
He grows strong.

Why should the light which flickers
in newly opened spirit of corn
go out?

I am the tender corn.
Your god is coming to you
from your mountains, over the ridge.

My life
is dawning
on me,

he grows stronger
he is born, once more

who is sun shining through rain
who is strongest
who is bravest in fighting surrounded by his enemies.'

55 *Song to the Snake-Girl, Chicomecoatl*

So many kernels on an ear of corn! Get up!
Wake up! You're our mother.
Don't leave us! We'll be orphans:

don't die, don't disappear to Tlalocan,
to that hidden realm of rain and mist.

So many kernels on an ear of corn!
Wake up! You're our mother.
Don't leave us! We'll be orphans:

don't die, don't disappear to Tlalocan.

56 *Song of Macuilxochitl*

Here I am
straight from

where the flowers are moist with dew.
I'm dawn lighting up the sky

like a soft wind stirring
as you,

the land, the mother
also are lady of dawn

as the stars in the sky
also know
what will come, they too

wind which will nourish,
the light of dawn slowly
growing

in answer to
tasselling corn . . .

[*the rest of the poem is lost*]

57   *Cure for a Love Spell*

Come!
here to me

woman in white
with your hair of smoke
your hair of mist,
your lush jade skirt,
mother, your rustling

Come!
here to me.

Watch me,
dark love
white love
blue love,

I've arrived, I am
the priest who owns the charms.

Mother, you,
whose skirt is stars:

did you do it?
did you put it in him?
earth

blue heart of rain, white heart of rain,
we're one as we writhe
together.

You did it!
You put it into him!

He's
at your feet.

3
Myths and Legends

Lady of the white jade skirt,
when your four-hundred offspring,
the cloud-snakes, northern stars,
were born, they fled and hid
in caverns of the earth.
Then you bore again,
this time five offspring, named
Eagle-Serpent
Cloud-Serpent
Wolf-Woman
Mountain-Hawk
Lord of the Canal.
They entered the water at birth,
stayed four days in the water
to fill out, and grow strong.
When they emerged, our Lady of the Earth,
you fed them from your breast.

The Sun gave his arrow
to the four-hundred cloud-snakes,
commanded them:
    'Take the shield and arrows.
    Find me drink and tribute!'
The arrow! It was precious,
made from sheaves of green quetzal feathers,
white plumes of the heron,
the zacuan's sunflower feathers,
pink from the redbreast, red from the troopial,
blue-green from the turquoise bird.
The Sun said:
    'Also remember your duty
    to the Lady of the Earth.'

But the four-hundred cloud-snakes
forgot their duty,
wandered hurling arrows at the birds,
gave their hearts and hands to pleasure . . .
If they killed a tiger, they did not give it
to the Sun, though they dressed up in robes
to celebrate the deed. Their one pastime
was to dress themselves in plumage of the birds
and lie beside their women.
Their wrong was even greater than this:
for they drank the cactus wine,
wandered always half-crazed, overwhelmed with wine.

The Sun frowned. He called
the five offspring of Our Lady.
He gave to them an arrow made of thistles, thorns,
a shield like that the noble princes wear.
He said,
    'My children . . .
    you must kill the four-hundred cloud-snakes.
    They have failed to call upon
    Our Lady and Our Lord.'
The five went to their duty, hid in an acacia tree
in ambush. The cloud-snakes,
seeing them within the tree, asked one another,
who was hiding there? Battle broke out then.
Eagle-Serpent slid into the body of the tree.
Cloud-Serpent dissolved into earth's body.
Mountain-Hawk became the mountain.
Lord of the Canal perched on the water.
Wolf-Woman, their sister, went to Tlachtli,
took her stand in the sacred court of the ball game.
The cloud-snakes circled the acacia tree:
the enemy was nowhere.
With their bodies the four-hundred

wove a hunting net, cracked the tree-trunk
with pressure from their bodies.
Eagle-Serpent leapt free
from the splinters of acacia:
the earth was set trembling.
Cloud-Serpent leapt from the entrails of earth.
The mountain burst with the din of landslide, fell,
and Mountain-Hawk leapt free.
The waters churned and boiled
and Lord of the Canal leapt from them.
Together, these four vanquished the four-hundred,
sacrificed them to the Sun, so as to drink their blood.
A few of the four-hundred survived,
came begging to the victors:
    'We have made you angry.
    But march now to Seven Caves,
    for they are now your caves.
    Enter your new palaces of earth!'
    'Are they really ours? Are they to be our home?'
    'You have won them in fair battle. They are yours.'
    'Then we shall sit in peace within the mouths
    of our own caves, our Seven Caves.'

One day two hinds came down from the mountain,
each hind with two heads. Behind them,
Precious-Turquoise and Arrow-Fish,
two survivors of the four-hundred, stalked.
They had wandered hunting on the rocky land
hoping to snare the two-headed hinds.
A whole night, then a day they trailed them,
until both hinds and men were weary. One hunter said,
    'Let us make two huts, one here, one there.'
When the huts were built, they said,
'Still the hinds do not come.'
But they came suddenly – those who had been hinds

were hinds no longer. They had become two women,
beautiful, who cried out,
    'Precious-Turquoise, Arrow-Fish, where are you?
    Come to us! Come eat and drink!'
The hunters called them. Precious-Turquoise shouted,
    'Come, sister, come here!'
One woman came to him, saying,
    'Drink, Precious-Turquoise!'
He drank the blood she offered,
then lay beside her, pressed her body
with his body, bit her lips, at last
entered her. He said to Arrow-Fish,
    'I have eaten what is mine.'

The second woman called to Arrow-Fish
    'Come, my lord, come eat!'
But he did not call to her. He made a fire,
and as it flared he cast his body in.
The woman followed, threw her body on him.
The divine cactus bowl came down from heaven
and the woman threw her body into it . . .
One of the Upholders of the Sky
saw the bowl was falling,
immediately hurled darts at the woman.
She leapt free, fled,
ran plaiting her hair, painting her body
as she ran, weeping that her lord
had been consumed by fire.

The gods, who made the years, heard of this,
hurried after her, to catch the woman
who was Obsidian-Butterfly. Arrow-Fish
ran before her. The gods caught up with her,
began to burn her body as she screamed.
From herself she hurled like sparks

numberless bright flints.
First the blue flint burst and flowered by her.
No one took it up.
Next the white flint burst and flowered.
Cloud-Serpent caught it up, bundled it away.
Then the red, the yellow, the purple flints
sprung from her body, burst and flowered.
No one took them up.
But Cloud-Serpent had the white flint
in a bundle for his god, packed it on his back.
He went off to his victories.

Cloud-Serpent went to capture the town of Huiznahuac.
On the road he met the woman Chimalman.
She came before him without robe or shawl,
naked, in her body. Cloud-Serpent did not look.
He fixed his shield, took four darts in hand,
cast them at Chimalman.
The first flew above her;
the second struck her flank; it was deflected.
The third she caught up in her hand.
The fourth skipped past her,
fell among the agaves.
Cloud-Serpent threw four darts
and fled along the road.
The woman fled too
to hide in a place called Red Cave.

Cloud-Serpent came again to find her, in his fine robes,
to hurl darts. He went to her town, Huiznahuac,
saying to the women of Huiznahuac they should find her . . .
In Red Cave they discovered her, said to her
    'On your account, Chimalman, Cloud-Serpent
    violates your sisters.'
They forced her to Huiznahuac. Cloud-Serpent

once again beheld her, naked as she stood,
but now her body painted red and yellow.
He prepared his darts. He overcame her with them . . .
he lay with her at last.
Cloud-Serpent left her with his child.
Fiercely the child struggled
four days in her womb. When he was born,
she died. The child was male,
named One-Cane. Quilaztli, Lady Serpent,
brought him up at her hearth,
and when he was old enough for war
she took him to contend against his father.
He learned to fight in the Place of Turquoise.
There too he learned to hunt, and there
his four-hundred uncles, the cloud-snakes lived.
They had come to kill his father,
whose body they had buried in the sand.

One-Cane searched everywhere for his father.
The vulture heard him asking, said,
    'Your father has been murdered.
    He is buried in the ground.'
One-Cane dug up the body, laid it in a temple,
the temple of Cloud-Serpent on the hill
of Cloud-Serpent . . .
Three of his cloud-snake uncles came to One-Cane.
They had murdered his father. They criticized him:
    'Why have you made a temple for your father?
    We will turn the hare, snake, tiger, eagle, wolf
    against you, they will punish you for this.'
The son replied,
    'What I do is right,
    what I do is right.'
He hastened all the same to call the tiger, wolf, and eagle.
When they came, he said,

'Uncles, it has been decided, you cloud-snakes,
I am to consecrate a temple with your blood.
But you will not die, my animals.
It is for you to kill and devour those
who gave me cause to build this temple,
killed my father. Devour them – it would be vain
to bring the victims roped together, back to back.'
Then he called the weasel to him.
   'Friend, we will dig and tunnel out
   chambers in this temple I have made.'
The weasel made a passage through which One-Cane
climbed up to the summit of Cloud-Serpent's temple.
His uncles, the cloud-snakes, cried out,
   'Let us fire the beams above his head!'
When eagle, wolf and tiger saw them come
they roared, and One-Cane unexpectedly lit
the sacrificial fire. His uncles prepared to fight.
The first cloud-snake slid up the steep temple
but fell back again. One-Cane rushed on him,
split his skull with a stone. The other uncles,
furious, summoned the wild beasts with their flutes.
But the wild beasts came to kill them,
smother them with smoke of the burnt chili,
sting them, stretch their bodies out for torture.
They finally sliced their chests wide open,
squeezing out their hearts.

One-Cane Quetzalcoatl went to the land of the dead.
He came before the King and Queen of the Dead.
   'I have come for the precious bones
   you have in keeping.'
The King of the Dead replied,
   'Quetzalcoatl, what do you want them for?'
He said,
   'The gods are sad, and say among themselves

they do not know who will inhabit earth.'
The King of the Dead made conditions.
   'You will have the bones, but first
   you must sound my conch-shell
   and travel four times round my disc of jade.'
The conch-shell had no mouthpiece to be sounded.
Quetzalcoatl summoned worms to mine it,
the night-bee and the bumble-bee to enter it
and sound it with their drone.
The King of the Dead heard. He said,
   'Well done. Take the bones of man.'
But he whispered aside to his servants,
   'Go tell the dwellers here that he has come
   to carry off the bones of man.'
Quetzalcoatl overheard, said angrily,
   'It is decreed that I must take the bones.'
To his companion, Lady Quetzalcoatl, he whispered,
   'Tell the dwellers here that I must take the bones.'
And he shouted aloud to them all,
   'I must take the bones of man!'
He lifted up the bones, half of man, half of woman,
bundled them on his back, carried them away.

Again the King of the Dead whispered to his servants,
   'It is true, true, he has come to carry off
   the precious bones. Run, dig a trench before him,
   he will fall!'
            They did this.
Quetzalcoatl, startled by a burst of quail-flight,
tripped and fell into the trench they made.
He lay as if dead, the bones scattered about him.
The quail began to peck and riddle them.
Quetzalcoatl came back to his senses, wept,
spoke to his companion,
   'Friend, how can this be?'

She replied in tears,
     'How can this be? How can this be?'
Quetzalcoatl gathered up the broken bones,
piece by piece, made a bundle of them,
and carried them upon his back to Tamoanchan,
the Place of Making.

When he came to Tamoanchan,
his companion, his Lady Serpent
Quilaztli Cihuacoatl, washed the splintered bones
in a precious glazed bowl.
Over them Quetzalcoatl bled his penis.
All the gods came then, five more beside Quetzalcoatl . . .
and bled themselves. For this reason we say,
     'Man was born of the gods',
because for us the gods shed their own blood.

The gods asked one another,
     'What will men eat?'
They began to search for corn . . .
Then the ant went to eat scattered grains of corn
on the Hill of Our Sustenance.
When Quetzalcoatl came upon the ant, he asked,
     'Where have you found corn to eat? Tell me.'
She would not reply, though he entreated her.
At last he touched her heart, she showed him
because Quetzalcoatl became a black ant,
conspired with another of that kind.
They forced the red ant to show them to the grain.
Quetzalcoatl took the grain to Tamoanchan
where the gods ate it, setting this word
on our half-formed lips,
     'We grow strong with corn.'

They asked,

'What shall we do with the Hill of Our Sustenance?'
Quetzalcoatl strained to lift it on his back,
tying it with ropes, but failed. Then it was
that Oxomoco cast the grains like dice,
gambling with Cipactonal . . . When they had cast,
the rain-gods heaped great clouds above the earth:
blue gods like the bare sky, white, red and yellow gods.
The syphilitic god struck the hill, and rain-gods
caught the grains of corn, corn of many colours,
white, turquoise, purple, yellow; and other food:
beans, wild amaranths, lime-leaved sage and argemone.
They gather from the air whatever feeds us.

Now Quetzalcoatl contended with the gods of rain
in the Ball Court. They asked him to set the stakes.
     'My precious stones, my feathers.'
They said,
     'We will risk our precious stones, our feathers.'
Quetzalcoatl won the game. The rain-gods
changed their stakes. Instead of precious stones
they gave the tender ear of corn;
instead of quetzal feathers they gave green leaves
of the seeding corn. Angrily, Quetzalcoatl complained,
     'Is this what I have won?
     These are not gems or plumes!
     Take them away.'
The rain-gods said to him,
     'As you please.
     Give him jewels and rich feathers.
     We will take away our precious stones
     which are the grains of corn;
     our plumes, which are green leaves.'
They went off saying,
     'We will hide our gems and feathers.
     Four years of famine will possess the earth.'

Then Quetzalcoatl was sad.
He thought back over how he had to go,
to leave his city, Tula. He thought of it
once more, and was determined.

They say he buried all: his shining gold,
smooth coral, and all else,
everything which was the richness of the Toltecs,
the artists. The precious things,
those we marvelled at, were all buried.
He put them all beneath the earth,
in underbrush,
in watercourses, deep in canyons,
inside the mountains.

The trees of fragile yellow cacao flowers and fruit,
the birds we treasured, in their plumes of solar fire,
left. He sent them on ahead of him
to the edge of the ocean.
And they went there.

Then he began his journey. And he came to a certain place
with a tree beside it, a fat full tree which springs up high.
He stopped beside it and saw himself.
He saw himself in the mirror and said,
    'I am old already',
and called the place
the Place Next To The Tree Of The Old Ones.
And he threw stones at the tree, a mosaic of stones;
the stones encase the tree,
then stay there as bark which covers the living tree.
It is how he saw himself in the tree,

root growing, lifting up into the crown.
As he went on his way, they were playing flutes.

Later, he came to a certain place
and sat down on the stone, leaned back on his hands:
as though the stone were clay,
the print of his hands stayed on it.
In the same way, the print of his buttocks on the stone
where he sat remained, gilded the stone.
It is how he saw himself: as the print of empty space on stone
which they called, 'Where There Is The Mark Of Someone's
Hands.'

And he turned back towards Tula and cried.
His body shook, shuddering, twisting like a thundercloud
as he cried. His grief became
twin plumes of hail, tears down his face,
cutting the rock as they landed, fell,
piercing the stone.

60 *Quetzalcoatl Changes Form*

And it is said that
he reached the edge of the sea in the year One-Cane.
He reached the beach of the great ocean.

He stood up
and began to cry.
He began to dress himself,
to put on the sacred clothing:
his green plumes of quetzal,
his sacred mask.

And then he stood up straight
and caught fire, set himself on fire,
and the flames embraced him.

And we know that when he burned
and his ashes flowed upward into the sky
all the birds whose feathers shine
came to see him, to watch –
all the birds who fly through air,

macaw with red plumes, indigo plumes,
the thrush with dappled feathers,
shining white bird, and the blue,
green, and yellow parrots –
all the most beautiful birds.

And when the ashes burned no more
his heart was at the zenith
and he was then called
'The Ruler of the Dawn.'

And we know besides:
he was not seen for four days, as he had gone
to the realm of the dead — he returned
with arrows in his fist, and after eight days
he became a great star.

And they say
it was only then
his reign began.

61 *The Fall of the Toltecs*

That shaman, owl man,
dressed himself in shining yellow feathers
once he had won. Then he planned that the people
should come together and dance.

So the crier went to the hill
and announced the dance, called out
to all the people. Everyone heard
and went straight to Texcalapa,
that place in the rocky country.

They all came, both nobles and the people,
young men and young women,
so many they could not be counted,
there were so many.

Then he began his song.
He beats his drum
again and again.

They join him in the dance,
they leap into the air,
they join hands and weave themselves
together, whirling round,
happily, happily.

The chant wavers up and breaks into the air,
returns as echo from the distant hills
and sustains itself.

He sang it, he thought of it himself,
and they replied.
As he planned, they took it from his lips.
It began at dusk and went on half way to midnight.
And when their common dance reached its climax,
numbers of them hurled themselves from cliffs
into gullies. They died, became stones.
They fell in the rapids and became stones.

The Toltecs never understood what happened there;
they were drunk with dancing, blind,
and afterwards they gathered there to dance
many times. Each time there were more dead,
more had fallen from the heights
into the rubble,
and the Toltecs destroyed themselves.

I myself am the enemy.
I search out the servants and messengers
of my relatives
who are dressed in dark plumes,
who are plumes of rain.

I have to see them here,
not tomorrow or the next day.

I have my magic mirror with me
smoking with stars,
and my allies

until those others, my relatives, those
dark plumes of rain in glistening sun

until they're put away.

4
Songs of War

63

Heart, have no fright.
There on the battlefield
I cannot wait to die
by the blade of sharp obsidian.
Our hearts want nothing but a war death.

You who are in the struggle:
I am anxious for a death
from sharp obsidian.
Our hearts want nothing but a war death.

64

He
reliant on
the word
of the White Jackal
of Cohuacan . . .

seeking
flowers which make
drunkenness,
reliant on
our lord
the sun . . .

I too
it is said . . .

65

In spring the songs are not
of peace
the flowers not
of peace.

Everywhere is hatred.

66 *Ometeotl to the Warriors*

Where men rule
we rule,

it is the first law —

Sun, the mirror
which makes things shine and live
must war with night.

'They're going, they are ready!
Be drunk, be drunk,
warriors!'

It is our work,
it is the work
of the androgyne (who gave men life)

men do when they die
at dawn —

sun, the shining mirror to them,
making all things live.

67

Now we are convinced
the priest Cuauhtemoc ...

   . . .

Your heart spins around
noble Cuauhtemoc,
it is war, the eagle,
the earth convulses in his claws,
the sky spins around.
It's that he's been abandoned:
the barbarians' Deer-Man.

68

Flowers from the marl,
blossoms of plumage
made men's hearts
straight.
But the eagle's war flower
bent the hearts of men.
  And war princes passed
  away.
  Kings became bright
  hummingbirds.

. . .

No one perceives
the shield-flowers wither.
  We must go elsewhere, nowhere,
  move aside, make room for others.
  Earth is a loan to us.

. . .

A lily of wind,
the spinning shield —
dust like smoke rises.
The warriors' whistle
sounds in Tenochtitlan!

69

While the chiefs pass their time
in games

don't be last.
Your fortune is war.

The sun rises up at dawn
like an eagle.

He knows where
his life is.

70

Sunflower, flower of shields
spins around, rich, sweet-smelling
flower. It's in our hands
here, by the shimmering water,
in a plain flowing like water with men,
the god will pick them, flowers.

71

Sacred crazy flowers,
flowers of bonfires,
our only ornament,
war flowers.

72

How do they fall? How do they fall?
These hearts, ripe fruit for harvest.

Look at them,

these fall, the hearts —   oh our arrows
these fall, the hearts —   oh our arrows

None so strong, none so prized
as the eagle in flight,
the tiger whose heart is a mountain:
    they submit to serve.
The yellow tiger weeps.
The white eagle forms a war cry
through his hands.
These are the princes . . .

There was the shaping of eagles,
making of tigers – the princes.
    There was a plain of battle
where the tigers learned their colour,
where the eagles swayed.
    A place
where Ipalnemoani
takes whom he will . . .

74 *Song of Warriors*

Princes,
eagles and tigers, into each others' arms
while the shields sound, they come together
to the festival.
There will be captives.   *y yao ay yaha*

They are scattered, they fall on us,
the flowers of war which are used
to please the giver of life, the sun.

Where it is boiling, where everything is upturned,
in the place of war,
where there is glory to have,
place where the rattles sound,
where a cloud of dust opens up.   *ohuaya ohuaya*

The flowered war need never end; it stays
by the river: there
the tigers as flowers,
the flowers of shields, have opened their petals,
there, in the place where rattles sound.   *ohuaya ohuaya*

There is the sweet garden of tigers: they will fall
in the midst of the plain.
They will pour their fragrance over us,
on us who wish glory and fame.   *ohuaya*

The ungrateful flowers, those flowers of hearts
have sprung up on the battlefield, at the edge of the fight
where the princes find honour and glory.   *ohuaya*

The shields of eagles mesh with the standards of tigers.
Shields with green quetzal feathers are given out.
The helmets, with gold-coloured plumes, moving like a snake,
shaking there in the boil, and the Chalca and Amaquemecan
    warriors
leap into battle, they who came, together, in great confusion.
    ohuaya

With a sharp noise
the arrow broke,
its obsidian point splinters,
upon us
the dust spreads,
is boiling.   *ohuaya ohuaya*

75

Where are you going? Where are you going?
To war, to the sacred water.
There our mother, Flying Obsidian,
dyes men, on the battlefield.
The dust rises
on the pool of flame,
the heart of the god of sun is wounded.
Oh Mactlacueye, oh Macuil Malinalli!
War is like a flower.
You are going to hold it in your hands.

76

Rattles shake the plain
where Tlacahuepantzin was left behind:
with yellow flowers
he is going to sweeten the realm of death.

You are only hiding in the north,
in Seven Caves,
where acacia grows, where the jaguar howls,
where the eagle roars, where everything is made.

You are the quechol, flame-coloured,
where you fly over the plain,
through the realm of death.

77 *Homage to Tlacahuepan*

With shields, you paint nobility.
With arrows, you write battle.
Now, you dress yourself in plumes
and paint your face with chalk for the sacrifice.
Oh Tlacahuepan,
you are going to take them with you into the realm of
    mystery.

Oh Tlacahuepan, you are over the princes.
You cry out, the eagle who is red answers you.
Like a dancer, who is to die,
with whistling hands,
and at the end, to the realm of mystery.

Your song is like a mottled jaguar.
Your flower is like the spread wings of an eagle.
Oh my prince, as a dancer, who is to die,
there in the clash of shields.
How beautifully you play your drum.

You garland the nobles with flowers of the eagle,
the gathering of friends, oh dancer, who is to die,
the wine of precious flowers makes men drunk and brave
and he will dress himself with his flowers and songs
in the realm of mystery.

Perhaps the Mexicans are singing there too.

78   *Elegy for Tlacahuepantzin*

God of rattlesnakes!
your flowers tremble —
tiger, eagle warriors roar.

The War Prince befriends
and favours us. But flowers
of flesh wither.
There, by the drums,
they are shuddering like women.

The war-dead! in the flowering water
with shields and banners raised!
Not by spears or arrows
the precious flower falls.

The flower made of human body
will never taint the moss
of Moctezuma, will not ever
sprout again in Mexico.

Smoke-stained, your red bird of light:
you pass, prince Tlacahuepan.
Smoke-stained, the god renews him.
God, god tears your flesh away!

. . .

. . . desolate my heart,
I see a child
tremble like a feather
shattered.

I go to the garden
where princes
make each other proud with flowers.
I see a child . . .

Drunk,
my heart is drunk:
dawn
and the zacuan bird is singing
over the shield stockade,
stockade of spears.

Tlacahuepan, neighbour, friend,
rejoice! You with your shaven head
are like one of the Cuexteca tribe —
drunk with the flower waters,
by the shore of bird-river,
with your shaven head.

Rocks fracture
jewels, precious feathers,
my princes:
those who were drunk with death
in the plain of water,
on the shore — there,
the Mexicans among cactus.

The eagle screams,
warrior with the tiger's face roars,
O prince Macuil Malinalli;
there in the field of smoke,
field of red . . .
it is right, it is right
the Mexicans make war!

.   .   .

My prince
blood-stained, death-yellow
the lord of the Cuextecas,
his skirt now black as the zapote fruit.
The glory of war clothes my friend
Tlacahuepan — in the mystery
where one perhaps lives on.

My prince
Matlaccuiatzin is drunk
with the flower of war, death-yellow
lord of the Cuextecas,
bathed in the liquid of war.
Together they go
where one perhaps lives on.

Sound the tiger's trumpet!
Eagle on the war-stone screams,
there on the carcasses of our dead lords.
The old men pass, Cuextecas
drunk with the flower of shields.
In Atlixco they dance!

Sound the turquoise drum.
Cactuses are drunk with fallen flowers;
you with the heron head-dress,
you with the painted body.
They hear him, go beside him,
birds with flower-bright beaks
accompany the strong youth
with the tiger shield. He has returned to them.

I weep
from my heart, I, Nezahualpilli.
I search for my comrades

but the old lord is gone,
that petal-green quetzal,
and gone
the young warrior.

Let the sky-blue be your dwelling!
Are Tlatohuetzin and Acapipiyol coming
to taste the water here
as I am weeping?

(*Nezahualpilli*)

80

I see the eagle and the tiger warrior.
Their glory saddens me who will depart
from earth, from the friendship of warriors.

Ipalnemoani,
you fly to us, bird
with a sword in your claw
and darts. Perched
in your own temple you preen
and sway among the drums.

Rain of down:
like a sacred heron you preen
and sway among the drums.

You tint the fire
and colour the throne of warriors.
My friends, you are princes
in the springtime palace.
What does Ipalnemoani require of us?

You will not remain long
in this palace. Nezahualpilli,
our friend, deserts you. War
sends up its flowers. Some grow,
some wither. They are eagles, tigers of war.

Those that wither
come back to you,
Ipalnemoani.

A march of warriors
to the region of Death:
every lord descended
but returned
in a flash
to live in the face of the sun.

Now they wander
the endless plain of the dead.

81

They look with envy,
they look with anger
at Huexotzinco.

It is surrounded with thistle swords.
It is blockaded with arrows,
the city of Huexotzinco.

Metal gongs and drums of tortoise-shell
roar in Huexotzinco.

But Tecayehuatzin and Quecehuatl rule there,
and flute and song ring out in Huexotzinco.

82

With upturned shields
we died in Chapultepec,
we died among the rocks.

The princes were borne off
in all four directions:
they are weeping at their fate.

King Huitzilihuitl,
a banner flutters in his hand
there in Colhuacan.

83 *Songs of the Fallen*

I (Prose Account of the Conquest)

This is how the Mexican, the Tlaltelolca perished. He abandoned his city. There in Amaxac we all waited. And we had no more shields, we had no more weapons, we had nothing to eat, and so ate nothing. And all night long the rain was falling on us.

II

As was their duty
they went slowly to the ruler and the judge
and were levied.

They sang only songs at Acachinanco,
to take heart
when they came face to face with the fires in Coyoacan.

III

We mourned for ourselves, our lot.
Broken spears lie in the by-ways,
we have torn out our hair by the roots.

Palaces stand roofless, blood-red walls.
Maggots swarm the squares and huts.
Our city walls are stained with shattered brains.

Water flows red, as if someone had dyed it,
and if we drink
it tastes of sulphur.

In grief we beat our fists
against the walls of our mud houses,
a net of holes our only heritage.

Our strength was in our shields
but shields could not resist this desolation.

We have eaten cakes baked of linnets,
chewed dog-grass that tastes of nitre;
we have swallowed lumps of clay, lizards, rats,
farm soil turned dry dust, even maggots . . .

IV

The lament extends like a cloud
and on the market town tears fall.
Already the Mexicans have fled across the lake.
They are like women. Everyone flees.

'Where are we going?'

'Oh, friends!'
and later,

'Has it happened?'

They have abandoned the capital already.
Smoke rises, the mist
is spreading.

Weep, my friends,
and know that by these deeds
we have forever lost our heritage.

Appendix

Poems from Contemporary Oral Tradition

Four Otomí poems

Yesterday it flowered.
Today it withers.

. . .

I am going says the cow.
I am going says the ox.
They are going down the mountain says the wasp.
I will follow them says the firefly.

. . .

The river goes by, goes by
and never stops.
The wind goes by, goes by
and never stops.

Life goes by
and never comes back.

. . .

Sun shines on a dewdrop:
it dries.
In my eyes, in mine, you shine:
I, I live.

Six Lacandon poems

Fishing for the Name of a God

I do this, I move my hand for him, whose name is in the sky, for him, whose name is in my hand. Don't let a false name in my hand. Take me, receive me, give me your name, do not let a false name in my hand. For him whose name is in heaven, in the house of stars, I say his name in the sky. Don't let my hand lie. Tell your name in the house of stars. Take my spirit in, into the house of stars. Take me. In this trunk, the root of . . . [the god] . . . For him, I say his word with my hand. Don't let my hand disappear. He tells the truth. He is finishing his word here in my hand. He will come up if it's well said. He finishes his word in my hand.

Purification of Grains of Copal Incense

Break! Split open! I burn you. Live! Wake up!
Don't sleep! Work! I wake you to life.
It's me who brings you up to life in the censer.
It's me who makes you fresh. It's me who builds your bones.
It's me who makes your head. It's me who builds your lungs.
I'm the one who builds you, your maker.

This sacred drink is for you.
This offering of *balché* is for you.
It's me who brings you to life. Wake! Live!

. . .

Every time I lift my foot,
every time I lift my hand,
when I move my tail,
I hear your voice from far away.
I'm almost asleep:
I look for a fallen tree,
I'm going to sleep in the fallen tree.
My skin, my foot, my head,
my ears, are striped.

. . .

I'm setting the virgin table
for you, god.
I offer you thirteen gourds, cool and virgin words.

Beans Offered to the Fire in the Name of the God

Here are the first beans.
I give them to you, god.
I will eat them.

Balché Offered to the Brazier in the Name
of the Gods

Take it yourself and enjoy it, take it with pleasure.
It is far away, the flavour of vanilla has gone away.
Take it and enjoy it, life goes over into you, breath
goes over into you. Take it happily, the smell of
vanilla is far away, the smell is gone.
vanilla is far away, the smell is gone.
vanilla is far away, the smell is gone.

Huichol Shaman chants

[These were collected by Fernando Benitez as he accompanied a group of shamans on their month-long pilgrimage to Viricota, the mythical centre of the world, where they will collect peyote — visualized as a sacred deer hunt — and communicate with the gods.]

Song of the Drunken Whirlwind

I'm invisible,
a whirling tree of air.

I can change myself
into a man or a woman.
As a man, I take women.
As a woman, I take men.

I'm drunkenness itself, the madman,
craziest madman in the world.
That's why they call me Taweakme,
the drunken whirlwind.

I can do a lot of things,
be bad or good — whatever!
I dress myself up,
with every kind of flower.

I can teach you to play the violin
but you have to put up with me —
that's the way I am — the drunk, the madman.
Don't pay attention to my ranting,
or to what I do or what I say.

I like to wander the edge of mountain cliffs,
jump from boulder to boulder.
You'll do better learning violin if you just go along.
Don't worry about me! No, no!
You won't go crazy from just a glimpse of me.
Don't be scared!

Cold night air swirls along with me,
a misty rainbow, wreaths of flowers,
flaming confetti arcs through the air,
the harvest, whirling yellow, shining magic dust!
I teach people to play the violin!

The Shaman's Lament

(ANTONIO BAUTISTA)

I went there, where
the hills can be seen.
I heard nothing. There,
where the hills
can be seen.
I didn't hear a thing. There was
nothing I heard.

(at the centre of the universe, there
where the true shape of the hills becomes visible,
no god of wind, no Blue Deer god
back empty-handed from the hunt,
stillness, silence)

Three Shamans' Songs of the End of the Peyote Quest

(HILARIO, HIS BROTHER EUSEBIO, HIS SON ANTONIO)

The flowered road goes here —
to Viricota, centre of the world
where spirits and humans mingle.

They say you are around
and I came to look for you.

Though I'm not like you, though I've sinned,
here I am, I came looking for you.

. . .

Viricota, Viricota,
who knows why
the roses cry?

Who can say? Who can foresee?
Who knows why
the roses cry?

. . .

Who knows why
the hills stood up in Viricota?
Who knows why the hills talk to us
here in Viricota, end of the peyote road.

First Peyote Song

There were the waves,
coming out from the waves, the sea,
and after the sea came the gods, all of them.

The gods passed by
like flowers blooming, shaped like flowers,
trailing behind the ocean waves.

And then they came to the world's placenta,
there where it springs out of the flesh of the womb
    which bore them.
And the cloud boiled up from the placenta.

And from the cloud, the heavenly temple,
and out of the heavenly temple, the deer who became
    corn
who was changed into cloud and then rained on the
    cornfields.

Ocean waves spoke to the gods
at the end of each of the paths
which go out toward the five ends of the world.

Out of the waves came the Blue Buck,
and Mari, the fawn who speaks to shamans,
and another multitude of deer.

Then on the altar
the arrow and the head of the deer appeared,
there on the mat of herbs.

The gods understood their messages —

the arrow that became cloud
and the deer's head that became rain.

So they went to the clearing made in the brush for corn
and that's where they left their offering.
They asked, what's happening here in the cornfield?

What's happening here, in the earth,
in the womb of our ever-changing mother?
We need to know what's going on!

So they hid in the mountains
and attended the heavenly birth.
They saw it all born:

sprouting from the altar, they saw
the shoots of cane, tender tassels of corn,
the ears of corn and round gourds.

The golden flower of the heavenly temple blossomed
and the gods picked it. They rubbed their huge hands together
making it into dust like pollen.

They used this to paint three sunrays on their faces.
They said this holy mat of wild herbs was the Deer's cradle
and now it will be his funeral pyre.

Because that's where they'll lay him down
when they kill him in the mountains.
They said that aloud just like that.

And then from blue waves came the Blue Deer,
lord of them all, standing up straight,
erect on the altar of the world that joins earth and sky.

In the north
in the south
in the east,
in the west,
blue deer became visible.

Second Peyote Song

The flowers are flying, spinning,
one turn around Burnt Hill
and fire, our father's father,
gives birth to the Deer and the altar.

The gods are talking!
They do talk to us
but no one knows what it means.

But here's the arrow. Look, you see it
piercing the centre of the prayer mat
speaking the language of the gods.

Next to the arrow, the snake, Blue
Jaikayuave interpreter for the gods,
who knows the arrow's language.

Prayer mat gives birth to the rain
unleashes rain and you hear
what the gods are saying:

Brothers, it's time to make the arrow of rain.
The knotted cord to mark passage of time
in our pilgrimage appears in the arrow's mouth.

Yet once again, the clouds boil up
and become the gods of each of the four directions.
They talk among themselves, they all agree:

Viricota
Aurramanaka, Tatei Nakawe
Tatei Urianaka, San Andres,

they all leap up in the air
and soar around the place
where all was born!

Descending once again to earth,
they see the arrow which marks the place
where the Deer was born.

They see the sacred prayer mat,
stretched out on it, our brother
Tamatz Kallaumari is resting.

Afterword

by Edward Kissam

Now, MORE THAN three decades after *Flower and Song* first
came out, this new edition provides an occasion to reflect, not so
much about these 'Cantares Mexicanos' (they stand for them-
selves), as about this small swirl of petals carried along in the
ongoing river flow of human language – how they came to us,
where they are in the geography of human experience, and
where they take us.

Half a millennium since European and pre-Columbian
Mexican culture first clashed in the Valley of Mexico, a
hundred lifetimes since the poets of Texcoco woke at dawn to
see Huitzilopochtli the shimmering hummingbird-like sun as a
warrior overcoming mist rising off lakeside marshes, there is the
temptation to relegate these poems collected by Fray Bernardino
de Sahagún to 'history'. But how close to home are they? Where
are they in the extraordinary mirror-dance of humans looking
at, 'reflecting', and sharing what they see of themselves and the
world? And what might they mean for our future?

Informed guesses are that truly human language has been
with us for 40,000 years and my own uninformed guess is that
some mode of literature – that is, words put together in such a
way as to be memorable, thought of as valuable enough to be
passed on from one to person to another, must surely have been
with us for at least half that time. So, these poems, preoccupied
with things passing, looking beyond the immediacy of day-to-
day life, are part of a grand, ongoing exploration and cognitive
explosion – transcending the constraints of gesture, miracu-
lously catapulting ourselves beyond pointing at what is imme-
diately before us, to affirm the lasting beauty of language, song
and drumbeats which, otherwise, fade into silence.

Still more ambitiously, the Nahuatl poets push toward a larger schema of the universe, the city of Tenochtitlan spread out as a 'flowered cloud', discerning the goddess in tasselling corn, the cloud-serpent in desert sky at night, capturing the dynamics of the ever-changing opposition of looming dark rainclouds and noonday sun. What we find in this cache of pre-Conquest cultural treasures, in contrast with some of the earlier explorations of language as a tool for creating history – the Sumerian tax records, the Mayan, Egyptian and other chronicles of lineages of powerful rulers – is language meant to last, more a 'natural history' of the way human beings consort with the world around them than scaffolding for mere financial and political accounting.

We first stumbled across these poems, songs, and chants Sahagún had salvaged from the post-Conquest efforts to destroy all prior local history and culture, when we were young American poets growing up in Mexico, when we were experiencing our own sense of cultural ambivalence about what mattered to us. Now, forty or so years after we first learned about them, we look at these 'Cantares Mexicanos' as having offered us a new pathway through the forest in seeking to find our own identities in a literary landscape which was then still fiercely Eurocentric. We are grateful to have been in the right place at the right time and to have the privilege of an opportunity to share these poems with an English-speaking audience.

We continue to be intrigued as we have learned still more about the diverse ways in which 'literature', those realms of language which somehow become sanctified and placed on the altars of countless syllabuses, is identified and disseminated. The long chain of transmission through which these poems from before the conquest of Mexico in 1521 were reborn in the twentieth and twenty-first centuries is a somewhat improbable one.

Without the sixteenth-century miracle of Sahagún's insatiable curiosity, his superiors' and predecessors' encouragement and the amazing decision to initiate the re-discovery of pre-

Conquest Mexican culture as a collaborative endeavour with the elders he gathered together in Santa Cruz de Tlaltelolco, this entire corpus would have been lost – as fleeting a marvel as the flowers and songs the Mexican poets likened to the flowers at the base of the mountains.

Without the lifelong scholarly work of Angel María Garibay, a respected classicist whose attention turned from Greece to focus on Nahuatl from 1940 until his death in 1967, we would quite likely not have found these original texts, archived deep in university and national libraries.

Without Ezra Pound's pioneering work in expanding the field of vision of English-language literature to dig down into a global spectrum of cultural histories and be illuminated by them, our ability to even perceive a broader spectrum of strategies for communicating human experience (such as those of the Nahuatl poets) would have atrophied.

Without the attention to Amerindian myth and oral tradition proposed by Gary Snyder, then expanded by Dennis Tedlock, Jerome Rothenberg and others, the English-speaking world's twenty-first-century sense of poetry in the new world would have retreated into the safety of poets' preoccupation with their own individual experience and been less willing to explore the more open field of language emerging from shared community perspectives. Yet, as we transition into a twenty-first century characterized by both a resurgence of tribalism and emergence of homogenized market-driven 'world culture', the challenge of understanding cultural diversity and how the prism of poetry configures both individual and, also, shared societal experience intensifies.

It is crucial to remember that the poems here are just a tiny remnant of the broad panorama of Amerindian vision, experience, and expression. As we move forward we will need to commit to much more than simply language rescue and cultural survival. We will need to affirm that the cultural universe – the enduring language and thought evolved from social experience

– is as broad and huge as the Milky Way.

We can easily imagine an alternate cultural universe in which 'flower and song' would be merely shards of anthropological curiosities. That points to another, final reflection. The enduring value of Nahua poets' oral tradition from half a millennium past reminds us that cultural diversity is the crucible of innovation. This body of poetry provides us an urgent reminder of the need to nurture fragile indigenous cultures, wherever they persist, in the face of the global onslaught of homogenizing instantaneous communication about fleeting trivia: Twitter, Facebook, instant-messaging. It is estimated that more than 3,000 languages will die out during the coming century. How many stories, how many enduringly shamanic poems sacrificed to the marketing buzz of here/now?

An inherent constraint on our translations of the poems, songs, and chants presented here is our linguistic and cultural distance from those who spoke them and our inability to adequately reconstitute the shared memories, actual experiences and the subtly shaded reinventions of experience which are both evidence as to how culture brings groups together and evidence of the formidable barriers to cross-cultural understanding. Inevitably, we have sometimes introduced into what might be seen as the archaeological record of language and cultural transmission our own modes of speech and cultural conventions.

Nonetheless, I believe the effort is worthwhile. At the same time, I urge readers to approach these poems, songs, and mythical accounts reflectively, as a starting point for their own ongoing efforts to capture the elusive multi-dimensional complexity of human experience. A foundation premise of writers' faith is that the aggregate of collective imagination and personal perspective which emerges in poetry makes it possible to transform the chaotic, vast kaleidoscope of human experience into a new and more elegant vision, rhythms and harmonies we can grasp and hold on to as we swim forward through time.

We will need to turn to these pre-Columbian singers, poets, and storytellers, but, also, to new, yet unborn singers for contemporary and future 'Cantares Mexicanos' to learn from others' chronicles of both day-to-day experience and metaphysical exploration how better to see, capture, and share ways of looking at our brief lives in the vast world of possibilities, to become singers scattering songs along the path.

July 2009

Afterword

by Michael Schmidt

IN THE 1970s and 1980s, poetry in translation seemed central to poets and readers alike: poets learned from the otherness of foreign writing; and they often found in the poetry of eastern Europe in particular a seriousness of thematic and historical engagement in which they felt their own poetry deficient. A whole discourse built up around notions of 'witness'. What was lacking in the quality of translations was made up for by an earnest worthiness in the enterprise and a sense that the conditions under which such poetry was written – under the censorship of repressive regimes, for example – gave it a moral authority that our comfortable, bourgeois poetry lacked. The strict judgment sometimes applied to original poems seldom extended to translations. Even today in many quarters it does not. I feel that it should, and translations – where they can be made at all – require something of a cultural context if readers are not to mishear, misread and even misappropriate them.

Some years ago I re-read (at the time, with dismay) my first book, *this* book, a joint venture with the American poet Edward Kissam, consisting of careful, much-debated translations from Nahuatl (Aztec and related) poetries. Nahuatl is a synthetic language, insistently polysyllabic, without prepositions, without pure sibilants, heavily consonantal. There is less a sense of words than of phrases, sense-bundles. There is no traceable link between Nahuatl and any European language.

Nahuatl poetry is the product of a sophisticated culture which itself draws on prior traditions and cultures. Its structures are strictly hierarchical in character and no *vox pop* finds its way into the rigorous formulae of the verse. Even the poems composed during and after the conquest are in a high style, which makes the fall they elegize all the more vertiginous. The poems that survive were taken down from dictation by clerical scribes in the years after the conquest of Mexico. These religious men (all men) transliterated the sounds they heard and did not always catch the sense; if they caught the sense they did not always catch the implication. Yet how close they were to the living source, and how clearly they heard the voices of their interlocutors, taking down what they said out of curiosity and also as an instrument of understanding and control.

Even though they were themselves children of the high baroque, the Spaniards did not respond to what later scholars describe as the integrated texture of a poetry in which each image, image pair or cluster contains figurative, religious, philosophical and literal meanings, conveyed with a rigour which makes the disciplines of medieval allegory seem almost elementary. The poetry subsumes in a developed oral 'code', fixed at the time of transcription, elements of cultures the Aztecs had swallowed up, especially the Toltec, and out of which they had themselves grown, especially the Chichimec. It can be read as a perversion of civilized Toltec values, yet those very values subvert the verse which – as a result – though celebrating war laments ephemerality, rejoices in brotherhood, and seems to run in the teeth of the prince-warriors who sang it. A limited number of stock images are used and they are capable of a range of meaning. Just as the scribes wrote down what they heard in partial ignorance of its meanings, so those who chanted and danced may not have savoured consciously the sedition in their mouths.

When I undertook my translations, my knowledge of the Nahuatl language was rudimentary. I used Spanish cribs *en face*, Spanish expositions, thin modern patristics, building a sense of the tradition through the filters of the language of men who had destroyed the larger culture, preserving almost accidentally, among so much other testimony, these verse shards. With gold, onyx, codices and other plunder, manuscripts were shipped back to Europe where they gathered dust in ecclesiastical and royal libraries for centuries. My particular advantage was that from a very early age I spent my spare hours visiting the ruins and haunting the Museum of Anthropology, first just off the Zocalo and then in its magnificent modern home in Chapultepec Park, so that I had an almost obsessive sense of the material culture out of which these words were still audible; I knew the huge stone gods and the little human forms, the toys and whistles, the serpents and the hummingbirds. I collected pre-Columbian ceramics and still possess a Totonac representation of Xippe Totec. It is possible to ballast a thin sense of the language with material weight; and I knew the Mexican landscapes because I self-consciously grew up among them.

There were real lessons in the poems for a would-be poet and apprentice-translator. I learned how one kind of poetry, remote from the kind I tried to practice, can contain and conduct meaning. Almost all the rules of modern poetry were broken by the Nahuatl poems which were at the same time, though formulaic, also remote from the poetry that Lord and Perry found among the Ramadan singers when they were exploring the formulaic orality of the Homeric poems. From the strangeness of Nahuatl prosody I learned something about their rhythmic strategy, its *otherness*. Working on these translations, especially once I had met Edward Kissam with his superior grasp of the originals and his much broader knowledge of modern poetry, advanced my understanding of how poetry might work, subvert and create. The experience could have taught me something else: that English was not always the most receptive host language.

At the time I still spoke and felt in a kind of American English; forty-five years later I speak and feel in a British, or a more narrowly English, English, and I have seen how that language is almost entirely unable to receive certain tonalities, certain forms. The balladic poetry of Antonio Machado and Federico García Lorca, for example, doesn't work in standard English. That most precise of languages excludes whole areas

139

of feeling and response. Donald Davie, a poet and critic from whom I learned a great deal as an editor and critic, writes in his poem from the early 1970s, a time of great tensions and uncertainty for him and his culture, the celebrated 'Epistle. To Enrique Caracciolo Trejo',

> *The English that I feel in*
> *Fears the inauthentic*
> *Which invades it on all sides*
> *Mortally.*

And he knows the perils that this fear entails:

> *The style may die of it,*
> *Die of the fear of it,*
> *Confounding authenticity with essence.*

The great inhibitor of responsible and yet expansive English writing is an irony which insistently attacks writer, reader and translator *in flagrante*, as it were. Deep feeling expressed in certain terms – archetypal, pastoral, balladic – can sound silly or false unless carefully stylized. And yet readers intensely distrust stylization in modern poetry, except when our greatest poets – Geoffrey Hill, Christopher Middleton and Charles Tomlinson among our senior contemporaries – bring off some magic which even ironic-we are not proof against.

What can an English reader learn from these translations which purport to be from the Nahuatl? Translations into lyric forms of what are elegiac, heroic and historical poems from a culture in which the lyric in the European sense did not thrive? Except for the 'Songs of the Fallen', poems of defeat touched with the rhetoric of the conquering culture and partly defracted through it, and translated (gratefully, I must admit) in collusion with it, how much comes across in English? Unless the reader is prepared to make an investment of study, goodwill and to suspend disbelief *au cœur*, how much comes through? Without foreknowledge of the nature of the language and tradition and of the accompanying ethnology, the poems can seem inert. Must the reader approach them by way of the introduction, led by the hand, in order to begin to adjust to the demands the poems make?

Approaching directly, the uninformed reader may discern the shadow of a poem within these translations. Ed Kissam and I have, I like to think, endeavoured to preserve a sense of their strangeness not only by keeping close to the economy of image and metaphor but also in creating a phrased lineation, stretching out the sense evenly through the line and the poem so that there are not those little *bon mots*, climaxes and lift-offs with which English poetry abounds, but a continuous process, a subordination of language and rhythm to the larger movement of the verse. Readers may feel that the translations begin to evoke cultural surroundings; it is to be hoped that the additional material provided – introduction, glossary and notes – may assist in making the poems, coming from so remote a culture, space and time, carry something that is distinctively theirs, rather than having been appropriated and colonized by another great assimilating language.

With the sound of the poems, and then the additional information, they can begin to be heard for what they are, though no British English form can convey them as experience in the terms they propose. There are no authentic instruments, as it were. And worse, we have lost the original notation because, like much ancient poetry, these verses existed in the context of music, occasion, dance and ceremonial. Most translations, if they get close to the literal (which is hard enough) tend to lose the figurative altogether, and it is the figurative that matters. These poems may come across as atavistic, primitive, absurd. Yet they are not absurd, not atavistic (on the contrary) and anything but primitive. By the time of Cortez their tradition stretched back perhaps seven hundred years.

Advancing age may have made me a pessimist. Perhaps in looking at these vivid poems which meant so much to me, I allow too little to the imagination of readers who come to Aztec poetry for the first time in English, and without the dust of Mexico in their throats. Perhaps there is too little of that dust remaining in my throat. When we read ancient Greek, or Chinese, or medieval poetry in translation, we know that we are far from experiencing the poetry in the way that its original readers or hearers did, or indeed in the way that it was intended. The same holds for Aztec poetry, only more so: because of the conquest, because so much was rigorously forgotten, there is no sense that this remarkable literature plays even indirectly into ours.

Many readers, aware of how much they do not know and aware, too, that the steps of the translator whom they are following are only slightly more secure than their own, still understand something – something that it is hard to name or paraphrase. Through such translations *a little* (a variable, perhaps, but not *nothing*) of value – from the simplest appreciation of the content of the poems to the suggestive nuances of the translator's approximation to the original – can be gained. A little, potentially an *explosive* little.

Translation into English from certain languages (as from certain specific poets) may be virtually impracticable. The closest approach is still remote; were it translated back into the original language, the result would be different in kind from the original text. If even where there are common antecedents and references translation can prove vexed, how much more so when the cultural break is complete? But the English-language reader can gain fragmentary access. And that *is* access: remote though the echoes are, they bounce off authentic surfaces and create the space for their otherness.

1996, 2009

Glossary

THIS BRIEF glossary attempts to define some of the more important allusions to people, places, plants and animals in the poems. It is not complete, but no major allusion is left unglossed.

ACACHINANCO   A city slightly south of Tenochtitlan (q.v.) in the Lake of Texcoco. It was connected by a causeway both to Tenochtitlan and Coyoacan (q.v.).

ACAPIPIYOL (ACAPIOLTZIN)   Tutor to Nezahualpilli (q.v.); an adviser to Nezahualcoyotl (q.v.).

AMAQUEMECA (AMECAMECA)   City near the foot of Popocatepetl, the volcano, near the border with the Tlaxcaltecans, traditional enemies of the Aztecs.

AMAXAC   A city in the Valley of Mexico, where many of the Aztecs fled when Tenochtitlan, their capital, fell to the Spanish.

ANAHUAC   Mexico-Tenochtitlan, the name means 'surrounded by water' in Nahuatl. It is used to refer both to the capital city and to the area of the empire.

ARGEMONE   A kind of poppy with a delicate white flower and characteristically thorny leaves, used in some Aztec medicines.

ATAMALCUALOYAN   A feast celebrated once every eight years. It derives its name from the ritual eating of 'water tamales', the unseasoned maize-cakes steamed in skins of the maize ear. The feast is probably associated with planting, and seems to have taken place at the conjunction of Venus and the Sun.

ATLIXCO   A city in the Valley of Puebla, over the mountains from the Valley of Mexico, where the Aztecs suffered a severe defeat at the hands of the Tlaxcaltecans.

AYOCUAN   King of Tepexic, also known as Ayocuan Xochimecatecutli. In the poem, Ayocuan is presumably a warrior, 'he who shot his arrow into the sky.' Another Ayocuan, King of Tecamachalco, is the poet referred to in the Dialogue of Poets which took place in Huexotzinco (q.v.) Three of the poems in

Cantares Mexicanos, some of the finest, are attributed to the latter Ayocuan.

AYOPECHTLI   Aspect of Chalchiuhtlicue, goddess 'living in the turtle's nest' at the edge between land and water, thus presiding over the transition from watery womb to daylight.

BALCHÉ   An intoxicating beverage made from the bark of a leguminous tree (*Lonchocarpus violaceus*) and honey-fermented. The Lacandon consider drinking it as part of shamanic homage to the gods who first made it, first drank it, and taught humans its preparation.

BALL COURT   The sky; the ball game enacts the mythical struggle of Huitzilopochtli and Tezcatlipoca, the sun and the 'smoky shield' of the night sky.

BLUE DEER   The primary deer deity, Tamatz Kallaumari, Lord of the Animals, Great-Grandfather Deer Tail, is visualized as emerging from the flames or appearing out of thin air, being also the deity of the wind.

CACAMATL   Son of Nezahualpilli, last king of Texcoco.

CACAMATZIN   Cacamatl Cuauhtli, poet, noble of the city of Chalco.

CHALCA (adj.)   Those of Chalco, a city on the south-eastern shore of Lake Texcoco.

CHAPULTEPEC   A hill of rock originally on the shore of Lake Texcoco close to the island city of Tenochtitlan, and strategic to the Aztecs for defence. Moctezuma's fresh-springs still flow there. The name means 'hill of the grasshopper'.

CHICOMECOATL   Seems to be the aspect of Chalchiucihuatl, 'lady of jade', earth goddess of fertility, which is that of sterility. She was portrayed as a pubescent girl.

CHIMALMAN   Mother of Ce Acatl Topiltzin Quetzalcoatl (q.v.), of the town of Tepotztlan. She figures in the poem 'Cloud-Serpent' (poem 58). The father of her child was Mixcoatl ('cloud-serpent').

COLHUACAN (COHUACAN, CULHUACAN)   City south of Mexico-Tenochtitlan, one of the cities of the Valley of Mexico founded after the collapse of the Toltec empire in the late twelfth century, prior to the arrival of the Aztecs.

COYOACAN   One of the older cities in the Valley of Mexico, on the southern edge of Lake Texcoco.

CUAUCHINANCO   A city-state about a hundred kilometres east of Tenochtitlan. The name makes reference to its being surrounded by forest, as it is in the lush temperate forest where the central plateau of Mexico falls off into mountains toward the Gulf of Mexico. It was founded by the Chichimeca tribe several hundred years before the Conquest, but had by the sixteenth century been reduced to paying tribute to Tenochtitlan. It is now the town of Huauchinango.

CUAUCUAUHTZIN   Poet-prince, son of Tezozomoc, ruler of Azcapotzalco, near Tenochtitlan.

CUAUHTEMOC   Last Aztec king. He led the Aztec nation in active resistance after Moctezuma (q.v.) had been stoned to death while attempting to convince the people to submit to the Spaniards. He succeeded Tlacaelel, who died of smallpox. Cuauhtemoc's surrender to Cortés (1521) marked the end of the Conquest. He was later tortured and killed on Cortés's orders during the march to Honduras. His name means 'falling eagle.' Poem 67 refers to a priest of the same name.

CUEXTECA   Members of the tribe which lived in the land of the Huastecs, on the Gulf Coast. They wore their heads shaven.

DEER-MAN   Tlacamazatl, the priest, a magical warrior in the spirit-world. The reference in poem 67 to the barbarians' deer-man appears to relate as much to cultural history as to actual events. The 'barbarians' are the Chichimecs, who were in political conflict with the Aztec empire, and the deer-man is likely to be a shaman. The sixteenth-century sources specifically point to the Chichimec as using peyote – probably as part of an archaic Uto-Aztecan shamanistic tradition which persists to this day in Huichol ritual and cosmology where sun, wind, fire, deer, and peyote are linked.

DIALOGUE OF POETS   Tecayehuatzin (q.v.) brought together a number of poets at Huexotzinco, his city, for a dialogue

(*Cantares Mexicanos* f. 9–12). This meeting provoked perhaps the finest flowering of poetry of friendship and life, and many of the poems we have translated are from this happy occasion.

HUASTEC   The Huastecs were a tribe noted for their original handicrafts, but more important culturally, they were a source for many of the subversive fertility rituals and beliefs which were anathema to the Aztec establishment.

HUEXOTZINCO   A major city in the Valley of Puebla, from which much of the remaining poetry came. The Huexotzincans were hostile to the Aztecs. See also Tecayehuatzin.

HUICHOL   One of the most isolated tribes in Mexico, who speak a Nahuatlan language and live in the mountains of the Sierra Madre Occidental in the present Mexican states of Nayarit and Jalisco. They retain a culture largely unaffected by outside sources and are famous for their beautiful embroidery. Their mythology is rich and complex, concentrating on the relations between men, gods, deer, peyote, corn and water-goddesses of springs, rivers and lakes. It is very probably derived from archaic sources prior to the Aztec sun-cult. The Huichols have been studied in depth by Fernando Benitez who devotes the entire second volume of his *Los Indios de México* to them. There is also much information on them in Karl Lumholtz's *Explorations in Unknown Mexico*.

HUITZILIHUITL   The second Aztec king, ruling 1393–1417.

HUITZILOPOCHTLI   'Hummingbird (*huitzilin*) on the left / south (*opochtli*)' – the bright shimmering sun, also eagle (at midday) who engages in daily battle with night and darkness. He is also contrasted to Tlaloc, god of rain, another aspect of cosmic duality. This figure, whose mythology includes multiple over-lays of belief systems, cosmology, and historical references is the god of war – a deity adopted as particularly their own by the Aztecs as they wandered south conquering older settle-ments and tribes. Hummingbirds sipping the nectar from flowers are associated with the sun being nourished by the blood and hearts of sacrificial victims and warriors fallen in battle. See also Tezcatlipoca, Tonatiuh.

ILILIN (ILILLIN)   A flower.

IPALNEMOANI   'He for whom we live'. Also known as 'Tloque Nahuaque', the 'god of the immediate vicinity'. Ipalnemoani is a central philosophical concept in Nahuatl literature. As a mythical personality he represents the unity of all aspects of the universe. He is particularly significant to the 'Toltec' school of poets (see Introduction), among them Nezahualcoyotl (q.v.) and his son. At the time of the Conquest, these 'reactionary' poets were attempting to return to the purer, classical Toltec tradition which antedated the Aztec supremacy in the Valley of Mexico. It was typified by a persistent sense of ephemerality, a reaction against the war-cult, and a seeking after permanence in friendship and beauty.

JAIKAYUAVE   The blue snake, also arrow, intermediary between spirit-world and the physical, visible world – helping shamans understand what they've heard from spirits, but also representing humans' prayers to the gods, as when the sacred quest for the peyote makes reference to 'hunting' the peyote, as deer are downed with arrows.

LACANDON   A small group of Maya living along the Usumacinta River in southern Mexico.

MACTLACUEYE   The Nahuatl name for the volcano now known as La Malinche in the central highlands north of the city of Puebla, 'She with the Blue Skirt', referring either to the springs that rise in its foothills or to the colour of renewed vegetation. See Mari Carmen Serra Puche, 'The Concept of Feminine Places in Mesoamerica: The Case of Xochiquetzal, Tlaxcala, Mexico', in Cecilia Klein (ed.), *Gender in Pre-Hispanic America*, Dunbarton Oaks Library, 2001.

MACUIL MALINALLI   A friend of Nezahualpilli (q.v.), who lamented him in his moving elegy after the Aztec defeat at Atlixco (poem 79). His name, derived from the date sign, probably of his birth, means 'five-grass-tuft'.

MACUILXOCHITL   Lord of flowers, games, poetry. His name means 'five flowers'. See also Xochiquetzal.

MATLACCUIATZIN   Mother of Nezahualcoyotl (?).

MEXICANS   i.e. Aztecs, called individually 'Mexica'.

MIMICH   See Xiuhnel.

MIMIXCOA   Cloud-serpents, identified with the Milky Way.

MOCTEZUMA (MOTECUZOMA, MONTEZUMA)   Moctezuma Xoco-
yotzin was the second Aztec emperor of that name (the first
was Moctezuma Ilhuicamina). A cultured and religious man,
he was taken prisoner by Cortés's plotting, while the Spaniards
were his guests. He was stoned to death by a mob in an attack
on the Spaniards' stronghold. He ruled from 1509 to July, 1520.

MONENCUAUHTZIN   Poet from the city of Huexotzinco (q.v.)
where the great 'Dialogue of Poets' took place in the palace of
Tecayehuatzin (q.v.).

MOTENEHUATZIN   Lord of Teupil, one of the poets at the
'Dialogue of Poets' at Huexotzinco.

MOQUIHUIX (MOQUIHUIXTLI) Lord of Tlaltelolco, a city near
Tenochtitlan, occupying a sister island to the great capital. His
wife, the sister of king Axayacatl of Tenochtitlan, had such
foul breath that her husband turned to his concubines for
pleasure. His wife complained, his mighty brother-in-law
grew angry, attacked Tlaltelolco, and annexed it officially to
the Aztec city. [León-Portilla]

NEZAHUALCOYOTL   1402–1472, King of Texcoco. He is the most
famous of the Nahuatl-language poets, considered by his
contemporaries to be the best master of the classical style.
Many tales are told of his wisdom as judge, public servant,
philosopher, and teacher.

NEZAHUALPILLI (NEZAHUALPITZINTLI) 1464–1515, King of
Texcoco, son of Nezahualcoyotl, and almost his equal in fame
as a poet. He was not so just a man as his father, suffering from
foibles like those mentioned in the note to 'Cuaucuauhtzin's
Sad Song' (poem 46). Four poems in the Cantares Mexicanos
are ascribed to him. His name means 'prince who fasts'.

NONOHUALCO (NONOALCO)   City of inhabitants of the Valley of
Mexico before the Aztecs' arrival; it was incorporated into the
metropolis of Mexico-Tenochtitlan.

ONE-CANE   Quetzalcoatl was said to have been born in the year
One-Cane (*ce acatl*). The Aztec calendar system typically
designates years with a composite name referring to the period
and the numerical sequence of the year during that period.

OMETEOTL-OMECIHUATL   Lord and Lady of duality; represented
graphically in the Codices as an androgynous god at the centre
of the universe, the navel, as the source of all other manifesta-
tions of deity. Perhaps to be identified with Huehueteotl, god
of fire, since fire had a dual and creative aspect as movement
(*ollin*), life in the interaction between heaven and earth. See
also Quetzalcoatl.

OPOCHTLI   A god associated with Tlaloc, visualized as ruling over
lake and marsh; inventor of net, spear-thrower snares and oars.
Probably birdlike himself, a tutelary spirit.

OTOMÍ   The major non-Nahuatl linguistic group in Mexico. These
poems were collected by Garibay in the town of Huizquilucan
in the mountains just outside Mexico City. The Otomís are
probably the tribes referred to classically as Chichimecas.

PLACE OF ORIGIN   Seven Caves or Tamoanchan (q.v.).

QUECHOL   Bird with reddish or rose-coloured plumage.

QUETZAL   Bird with long blue-green tail plumes, more highly
valued among the Aztecs than gold. The bird, native to Central
America, is now the national symbol of Guatemala.

QUETZALCOATL   The most famous of the Mexican gods, his name
is usually interpreted to mean 'plumed serpent'; he is identified
with the god of wind (Ehecatl) and with the planet Venus. As a
legendary prince, he was famous for his wisdom and asceticism,
until tempted by his adversary, Tezcatlipoca (q.v.), his stellar
opponent. Many of the poems translated, especially the long
narratives, recall his parentage and his development both as
God and as Lord of the Toltecs (q.v.). If there was a tendency
towards monotheism in pre-Columbian Mexico, it centred on
him – his name has recently been interpreted as 'plumed twin',
the god of duality, Ometeotl. His nature is complex, and in
him many divergent powers focus. See also One-Cane.

QUILAZTLI 'She who makes green things grow', the aspect of the Earth Mother concerned especially with the sprouting of plants. In her sexual aspect as a fertility goddess she is represented as an eagle with a mask encircled with blood; she is bloody, as women giving birth were often called 'warriors'. As Quilaztli Cihuacoatl she is earth-snake-woman, feathered in the leaves of young plants.

SAN ANDRES Saint Andrew has joined the earlier pantheon of Huichol deities, a reminder that robust cultures, spiritual beliefs, continually evolve.

SEVEN CAVES Chicomotzoc, the Place of Origin (q.v.) of the tribes. See also Tamoanchan.

TAMATZ KALLAUMARI Older Brother Deer/Lord of the Deer, protects hunters but may also lead them to their death. Shamans listen to him and think of themselves as translating what he says. He is central to the extensive family of deer deities but the shamans' spiritual journey is considered an arduous, dangerous one.

TAMOANCHAN Also known as Tlalocan, a mythical place, 'the house from which we descend', the place of creation. The souls of the dead live there as spirits. It is the region of mystery and at once the paradise of vegetation. Associated with Tlaloc, the rain god, it is swathed in mist, a place of fecundity. In it, the tree of life grows, and sometimes Ipalnemoani (q.v.) is said to live there.

TATEI NAKAWE Mother of the gods, reigning over the growth of vegetation and corn. She is also known as 'the one who makes trees sprout and be renewed'.

TATEI URIANAKA The world, conceived of as a shallow gourd which rests on its bottom and is surrounded by five seas. This gourd, conceived as a female deity, is also used to represent the idea of fecundity and is sometimes referred to as a metaphor for the womb (*urianaka*, literally, stomach, abdomen). The female earth is imbued with motherly attributes as suggested by the prefix *tatei*, mother (Anthony Alan Shelton, 'Huichol

Natural Philosophy', *The Canadian Journal of Native Studies* VII, 2 (1987): 339–354.)

TAWEAKME   Whirlwind, 'drunken wind', born from the *kieri* plant at the beginning of the world, a plant whose yellow dust can makes people dizzy or sick.

TECAYEHUATZIN   King of Huexotzinco, a poet, and host of the 'Dialogue of Poets', several fragments of which (*Cantares Mexicanos* f. 9–12) are translated in this book. Miguel León-Portilla argues in his excellent edition and translation of the text that Huexotzinco was the centre of a cultural renaissance which, at the time of the Conquest, had begun a cultural revolution against Aztec domination.

TEMILOTZIN   Aztec prince-warrior and poet, a hero during the Conquest when he fought beside Cuauhtemoc. As a poet, his duty was to encourage friendship through his song. Captured by Cortés's local vassals, he jumped into the sea. The Chronicles record: 'Temilotzin would not listen, would not be held back. They saw him throw himself into the water. He swims off towards the sun. Malintzin calls after him, saying, 'Where are you going? Come back! Come back!' He did not listen, he went away, disappeared. No one knows if he reached the other shore of the sea, if a serpent devoured him, a lizard ate him, or if a big fish finished him off . . . but this way he took his own life. No one killed him.'

TENOCHTITLAN   Capital of the Aztec empire, site of the present-day city of Mexico, the city 'surrounded by water' described by Bernal Diaz as a place of golden palaces equal in wonder to the romance of *Amadis of Gaul*. The city was set in the midst of Lake Texcoco, connected by causeways to the mainland.

TEXCALAPA   'The stony place'.

TEXCOCO   A major city on Lake Texcoco which held ascendancy before the Aztec arrival. It is the source of much of the remaining verse left to us. It was also the site of the last Aztec religious rising against Spain, and one of the first schools set up by the early friars was located there.

TEZCATLIPOCA   The god of sorcerers, eternally young. He is also known as 'the enemy' (cf. poem 62) and as a patron of warriors is associated with Huitzilopochtli, the sun and war god. Originally he symbolized the night sky, thus his name: 'the mirror that smokes'. One of the codices tells how he, jealous of wise Quetzalcoatl (q.v.), lured the good king into drunkenness and incest with his sisters. Then he showed him his face in the 'mirror that smokes', and the remorseful Quetzalcoatl migrated south and set to sea on a raft of rattle-snakes, or (in variant legends) built himself a pyre, burned his body, and left the world with the promise that he would return in the year 'One-Cane'. When that year came, Cortés arrived.

TLACAHUEPANTZIN (TLACAHUEPAN)   A ritual figure, a young man sacrificed at the feast of Toxcatl as one of the 'cloud-snakes' (cf. 'Cloud-Serpent', poem 58) who returns to the Seven Caves, place of Aztec origin. In 'Nezahualpilli's Lament' (poem 79) he was the king's warrior friend, killed in battle.

TLALOCAN   Place of Tlaloc, god of rain, an earthly paradise of flowers hidden in mountains. Cf. Tamoanchan.

TLACOPAN   A city-state situated on the western shore of Lake Texcoco. Tlacopan sided with Tenochtitlan and Texcoco in their conquest of Azcapotzalco, becoming a member of the Triple Alliance which ended with the Spanish conquest of Mexico by Cortés and his native allies in 1521. It is now called Tacuba.

TLALTECATZIN   A lord of Cuauhchinanco, a major Aztec poet, present at the 'Dialogue of Poets' at Huexotzinco.

TLALTECUHTLI   Earth goddess. Garibay cites the myth in which Quetzalcoatl and Tezcatlipoca brought her down from the sky and she fought so hard that her body was torn apart. To console her the gods ordered that 'they made trees and flowers and herbs from her hair, tiny flowers and grass from her skin, springs and small caves from her eyes, rivers and caverns from her mouth, and valleys and mountains from her nose.'

TLALTELOLCA (adj.)   The inhabitants of Tlaltelolco, a northern subdivision of the city of Tenochtitlan (q.v.).

TLAXCALA   City-state north of Tenochtitlan; the major opponent to Aztec hegemony in the north. Cortés found his best local allies here. The city was culturally rich and a centre of humane worship on the Toltec (q.v.) model. The first indigenous converts to Catholicism were made here.

TLAZOLTEOTL   The goddess of the earth. As Teteoinan, her name means 'mother of the gods'. As Tonantzin, she is 'our mother', the mother of mankind. In her aspect as Tlazolteotl, she is 'devourer of offal', since she fed on corpses, symbolized as hearts. As Coatlicue, 'the lady with the skirt of snakes', she represented the fertile earth.

TOLTEC   A Nahuatl-speaking tribe. Their capital was Tollan, and four centuries before the Aztecs arrived their empire extended throughout central Mexico. Their great achievements in art and architecture, poetry and astronomy, were widely dispersed, and later tribes looked back on them as a classical culture whose ideals were to be emulated, though the Aztec establishment frowned on their cult of Quetzalcoatl, their tendency towards humane monotheism. As an historical figure, Ce Acatl Topiltzin Quetzalcoatl was the ruler of the Toltecs, but it is hard to segregate the historical from the legendary figure in the lists of his exploits. He is said to have turned a nomadic tribe of barbarian warrior-plunderers into artisans, poets and philosophers in one generation.

TONATIUH   The sun of the current era, the fifth sun. One version of the creation myth suggests that Huitzilopochtli (q.v.) was the one of the gods arrayed around a bonfire who finally sacrificed himself by jumping into the fire to create Tonatiuh, the sun shining on the world humans live in.

TOTOQUIHUATZIN   King of Tlacopan (1431–1469). His name has the sense of 'rain of birds'.

TULA   The Toltec (q.v.) capital, Tollan.

TZINITZCAN   A brightly-coloured small bird, sometimes said to be the hummingbird.

VIRICOTA   Mythical place of origin for the Huichols, where all transactions between gods and man took place, and Tamatz Kallaumari (q.v.), pre-eminent deer god, comes to earth. The present-day peyote-gathering pilgrimage takes the pilgrims to an actual Viricota in the western part of San Luis Potosi.

XIPPE TOTEC (XIPE)   A Huastec (q.v.) god of fertility. He is represented as a priest wearing the flayed skin of his victim. In this form he represents the rebirth of vegetation in spring, and is associated with rain and moistness. He also represents sexual fertility, and as such is worshipped in the form of a phallus. As 'he who drinks night', seems also to be identified with the sun.

XIUHNEL *and* MIMICH   Two of the survivors of the four-hundred cloud-snakes, they are represented as hunters, each with two deer heads on his shoulders. Their names mean 'precious turquoise' and 'arrow fish' (cf. 'Cloud-Serpent', poem 41).

XOCHIPILLI   See Xochiquetzal.

XOCHIQUETZAL   Goddess of flowers and love, she is associated with rain and vegetation. Her husband is a young warrior, the sun, whose love she receives, conceives his children, innocent of the fact that they will be warriors. She is also associated with Xochipilli, who is more particularly a sort of Muse figure, presiding over 'flower and song' and dancing; and with Macuilxochitl (q.v.). Her own name means 'plumed flower'.

YOYONTZIN   Nezahualcoyotl.

ZACUAN   Bird with yellow or gold plumage.

ZAPOTE   A black fruit of the hard-wood zapote tree.

Sources

The main editions used in making the translations were:

BENITEZ, FERNANDO: *Los Indios de México*, Mexico, 1968

DURÁN, FRAY DIEGO: *Historia de las Indias de Nueva España* ...,
   (two volumes), Mexico, 1867, 1880

GARIBAY, ANGEL MARÍA K.: *Llave del Náhuatl*, Mexico, 1940
   Epica Náhuatl, Mexico, 1945
   Historia general de las cosas de la Nueva España, Mexico, 1956
   [his edition of the Florentine Codex]
   Historia de la Literatura Náhuatl (two volumes), Mexico, 1953
   Veinte himnos sacros de los Nahuas, Mexico, 1958
   Poesia Náhuatl (three volumes), Mexico, 1964 [his edition of
   the *Cantares Mexicanos* and *Romances de los señores de la
   Nueva España*, with a translation which forms the basis of
   most of the versions in this book]

LEÓN-PORTILLA, MIGUEL: *La filosofía Náhuatl, estudiada en sus
   fuentes*, Mexico, 1956
   Los antiguos mexicanos, através de sus crónicas y cantares,
   Mexico, 1961

POMAR, JUAN BAUTISTA: *Relación de Tezcoco* (1582), Mexico, 1891

SODI MORALES, DEMETRIO: *La literatura de los Mayas*, Mexico,
   1964

References

In these references, CM indicates *Cantares Mexicanos*, RS *Romances de los señores de la Nueva España* and VH *Veinte himnos sacros de los Nahuas*. The translator is indicated by his initials; where none appear, the translation is a joint version.

1	RS f. 17: MS
2	RS f. 20: MS
3	CM f. 17: MS
4	CM f. 21: MS
5	CM f. 25: MS
6	CM f. 15: EK
7	CM f. 19: MS
8	RS f. 35: MS
9	RS f. 7: MS
10	RS f. 16: MS
11	CM f. 22: MS
12	CM f. 67
13	CM f. 35: MS
14	CM f. 17: MS
15	CM f. 14
16	RS f. 16v: EK
17	CM f. 71: EK
18	RS f. 38: EK
19	VH 19 11. 15–22: EK
20	CM f. 12: EK
21	CM f. 30: MS
22	CM f. 19: MS
23	RS f. 2: MS
24	CM f. 2: EK
25	CM f. 22: EK
26	CM f. 9: EK
27	CM f. 35
28	CM f. 9: EK

29	CM f. 12: EK
30	CM f. 71: EK
31	CM f. 9–12
32	CM f. 13r: EK
33	CM f. 69: EK
34	CM f. 69: EK
35	CM f. 9
36	CM f. 22
37	CM f. 17: EK
38	CM f. 11: MS
39	RS f. 14: MS
40	CM f. 9–12: EK
41	RS f. 5: MS
42	CM f. 35: MS
43	CM f. 17
44	CM f. 10: EK
45	CM f. 9–12: EK
46	RS f. 26–7: MS
47	VH 4: EK
48	VH 5: EK
49	VH 7: EK
50	VH 9: EK
51	VH 12: EK
52	VH 13: EK
53	VH 14 i and ii: EK
54	VH 15: EK
55	VH 16: EK
56	VH 20: EK
57	VH appendix V no.3: EK
58	Sahagún's 'Anales de Cuauhtitlan' in *Épica Náhuatl*: MS
59	*Llave del Náhuatl* text 7: EK
60	Sahagún's 'Anales de Cuauhtitlan' f. 7: EK
61	*Llave del Náhuatl* text 5: EK
62	VH Appendix V no. 1: EK
63	CM f. 9: EK
64	RS f. 9: MS
65	CM f. 11: MS

66 VH Appendix I no. 1: EK
67 RS f. 14: EK
68 CM f. 20: MS
69 RS f. 42: EK
70 RS f. 8v: EK
71 RS f. 8v: EK
72 VH Appendix I no.3: EK
73 CM f. 20
74 CM f. 18: EK
75 CM f. 70
76 CM f. 22
77 CM f. 23: EK
78 RS f. 31: MS
79 CM f. 55–6: MS
80 CM f. 2: MS
81 CM f. 32: EK
82 CM f. 12: EK
83 *Cantos de los Vencidos* in *Historia de la Literatura Náhuatl*:
    MS (I, III, IV); EK (II)

Appendix

All translations by EK.

OTOMÍ POEMS: from *Historia de la Literatura Náhuatl*, vol. 1.
LACANDON POEMS: from Demetrio Sodi Morales, op. cit.
HUICHOL SHAMAN CHANTS: from Benitez, op. cit., pp. 136–7 and
    550–1.

Further Reading

The books listed (all in English, or English translation) are easily accessible to readers, either in libraries or from bookshops. They are only a few of the large number of important studies in the field. Those marked with an asterisk are possibly the most interesting and cogent.

BERNAL, IGNACIO: *Mexico Before Cortez, New York, 1963

BRINTON, DANIEL: Ancient Nahuatl Poetry, Philadelphia, 1887

CASO Y ANDRADE, ALFONSO: *The Aztecs: People of the Sun, Oklahoma, 1958

CLAVIGERO, F. S.: The History of Mexico, translated by Charles Cullen, two vols., London, 1787

DIAZ DEL CASTILLO, BERNAL: *The Conquest of New Spain, translated by J. M. Cohen, Harmondsworth, 1963

DURÁN, FRAY DIEGO: The History of the Indies of New Spain, translated, annotated and with an introduction by Doris Heyden, Oklahoma, 1994

FLORESCANO, ENRIQUE: The Myth of Quetzalcoatl, translated by Lysa Hochroth, Baltimore, 1999

FURST, JILL LESLIE MCKEEVER: The Natural History of the Soul in Ancient Mexico, New Haven, 1997

LEE, JONGSOO: The Allure of Nezahualcoyotl: Pre-Hispanic History, Religion, and Nahua Poetics, Albuquerque, 2008

LEÓN-PORTILLA, MIGUEL: *Aztec Thought and Culture: A Study of the Ancient Nahuatl Mind, translated by Jack Emory Davis, Oklahoma, 1963

*Pre-Columbian Literatures of Mexico, Oklahoma, 1968

LEÓN-PORTILLA, MIGUEL and SHORRIS, EARL: In the Language of Kings: An Anthology of Mesoamerican Literature, Pre-Columbian to the Present, New York, 2001 [Nahuatl, Mayan, Mixtec, Mazatec, Zapotec, Otomí, Purepecha, Tlapanec]

MARKMAN, ROBERTA H. and PETER T.: The Flayed God: The Mesoamerican Mythological Tradition, New York, 1994

MAXWELL, JUDITH M. *and* HANSON, CRAIG A.: *Of the Manners of Speaking That the Old Ones Had: The Metaphors of Andrés de Olmos in the TULAL Manuscript*, Salt Lake City, 1992

MILLER, MARY *and* TAUBE, KARL: *An Illustrated Dictionary of the Gods and Symbols of Ancient Mexico and the Maya*, New York, 1993, 1997

NICHOLSON, IRENE: *Firefly in the Night*, London, 1959
The X in Mexico, London, 1965
Mexican and Central American Mythology, London, 1967

O'GORMAN, HELEN: *Mexican Flowering Trees and Plants*, Mexico City, 1961

PADDEN, R.C.: *The Hummingbird and the Hawk: Conquest and Sovereignty in the Valley of Mexico, 1503–1541*, Columbus, Ohio, 1967

SÉJOURNÉ, LAURETTE: *Burning Water: Thought and Religion in Ancient Mexico*, London, 1957

SMITH, MICHAEL E.: *The Aztecs*, Oxford, 1996; 2nd edition, 2003

SODI MORALES, DEMETRIO: *The Maya World*, Mexico, 1976

SOUSTELLE, JACQUES: *Cosmology of Ancient Mexico*, London, 1957
Daily Life of the Aztecs, Harmondsworth, 1961

SPENCE, LEWIS: *The Gods of Mexico*, London, 1923

SPINDEN, HERBERT: *Ancient Civilizations of Mexico*, New York, 1933

STEVENSON, ROBERT: *Music in Aztec and Inca Territory*, Berkeley and Los Angeles, 1968; 2nd edition, 1976

THOMPSON, J. ERIC: *Mexico Before Cortez*, London, 1933

VAILLANT, G. C.: *Aztecs of Mexico*, Harmondsworth, 1952

CD-ROM

Códices de México: CD-ROMS 1–4 [Colombino, de Huamantla, Chavero de Huexotzingo, Huichapan]. PC only.